GOOD NEWS

For my wonderful grandmothers, Aaji and Maayi. R.S.
To Annie and Bill. A.H.

First published in Great Britain in 2021 by Wren & Rook
Text copyright © Rashmi Sirdeshpande 2021
Design copyright © Hodder & Stoughton Limited 2021
All rights reserved.

ISBN: 978 1 5263 6338 1
E-book ISBN: 978 1 5263 6339 8
10 9 8 7 6 5 4 3 2

Aston Martin ® is a trademark of Aston Martin Lagonda Limited. IKEA ® is a registered trademark of Inter-IKEA Systems B.V. LEGO ® is a registered trademark of LEGO Juris A/S. GAP ® is a registered trademark of GAP (Apparel), LLC. Play-Doh ® is a registered trademark of Hasbro, Inc. Slinky ® is a registered trademark of Poof-Slinky, LLC. Unilever ® is a registered trademark of Conopco, Inc.

MIX
Paper from
responsible sources
FSC® C104740

Wren & Rook
An imprint of
Hachette Children's Group
Part of Hodder & Stoughton
Carmelite House
50 Victoria Embankment
London EC4Y 0DZ

A Hachette UK Company
www.hachette.co.uk
www.hachettechildrens.co.uk

Senior Commissioning Editor: Laura Horsley
Art Director: Laura Hambleton
Senior Designer: Sophie Gordon
Senior Editor: Sadie Smith
Production Controller: Kelly Llewellyn
Designed by Kathryn Slack

Additional images supplied by Shutterstock

Printed in China
The website addresses (URLs) included in this book were valid at the time of going to press. However, it is possible that contents or addresses may have changed since the publication of this book. No responsibility for any such changes can be accepted by either the author or the publisher.

All facts and research are correct as of early 2021.

RASHMI SIRDESHPANDE

ILLUSTRATED BY
ADAM HAYES

GOOD NEWS

WHY THE WORLD IS NOT AS BAD AS YOU THINK

wren
&rook

CONTENTS

'THE WORLD IS GETTING BETTER

'ENDANGERED TIGERS MAKE AN AMAZING COMEBACK'

'KIDS ARE CLEVERER THAN EVER'

THIS is the kind of news we want to see. The moments of humanity, kindness and goodness in the world. And there's lots of it out there. But when you see the grown-ups watching the news or flicking through newspapers in the shops, you probably just see things that look bad. *Really* bad.

Imagine if you were an alien life form that had just beamed on to this planet (one that can somehow read and understand a whole bunch of human languages). You walk around for a bit, look at the streets, the buildings, the people and then you see a newspaper packed with terrible things – stories of crime and tragedy, stories about the planet being destroyed, stories about how everything is awful and it's only getting worse and there's nothing anyone can do to stop it. Would you want to stick around on this planet or would you beam straight back into space and get as far away as you possibly can?

I'm guessing you'd already be zooming off into space because the news tells us we're **DOOMED**.

BUT WAIT. THAT'S NOT THE WHOLE STORY. IT'S JUST PART OF IT.

In fact, can we hit pause for a moment on that word 'story'? It's important. That's what the news is. A story. When you think about stories in books and in films, what do you like to read and watch?

OPTION 1: The ones where *nothing* happens? Or stuff happens but it's really small, boring stuff and everything is basically very nice and then everyone goes to sleep? Or ...

OPTION 2: The *exciting* stories and the *exciting* films? You know the ones. The books you can't put down, the films you have to finish because you just *have* to know what happens.

Most people would pick Option 2. We like a good story. This is the thing about the news. It tells a good story. A gripping story. Whether we like it or not, sensational, scary stuff makes people sit up and listen. It makes them want to hear or read more. It sticks in their mind. It makes them want to *tell* someone about it. It makes *that* person want to tell someone *else* about it. And before you know it, a piece of news has whizzed its way around the world faster than you can say 'Bob's your uncle'.

This is why we end up seeing lots of that scary stuff and why we don't see so much of the **GOOD STUFF**. That's what this book is about. **GOOD NEWS**. Because it exists. *Lots* of it. It just doesn't get as much airtime because a lot of it is gradual improvements or small acts of kindness and people continuing to do good work, day in and day out – and, frankly, that just isn't as juicy as a hard-hitting headline about what a *disaster* everything is.

'PERSON CHECKS IN ON AND CHEERS UP ELDERLY NEIGHBOUR'

'GLOBAL CARBON DIOXIDE EMISSIONS THIS YEAR ARE THE SAME AS LAST YEAR'

The last one doesn't sound like a big deal, but it would be HUGE news. It would mean we used lots more renewable energy such as wind and solar power, and we *might* have hit the peak for emissions. Maybe they're going to fall after this.

That doesn't mean that some of that bad news isn't useful. Of course it is. We need to know what's happening in the world around us. How else are we going to make things better? It's about the balance of the news we gobble up. Right now, that balance is tipped in favour of the bad stuff.

Because we see so much more of the *bad* news, it's so easy to start thinking that things are much worse than they actually are. But we need to hear the *good* news so we can see how amazing our world truly is and the great part **YOU** have to play in keeping it that way.

WIRED TO WORRY

Now, you might be wondering why on earth we find bad news so interesting in the first place. The thing is, we're wired to worry ...

This is something humans have been stuck with because, many thousands of years ago, a bit of anxiety was just the ticket to stop us getting eaten. It was much better to see danger everywhere and jump at a shadow or the slightest noise and to keep *safe*, than to be overconfident and get gobbled up by a predator. But this means that now, negative stuff tends to affect us much more than positive stuff. It's where our attention goes, and it's the thing that sticks in our heads.

And there's another problem: our brain likes to take **SHORTCUTS** to save time and energy. Another early human thing. One shortcut the brain takes is to rely on information that springs to mind quickly. Because bad news is everywhere, we can often immediately come up with vivid examples of terrible things. And because we remember these terrible things so easily, they feel way more common than they actually are. For example, the images of shark attacks in the news are so vivid that people often think deaths by shark attacks are quite common. They're not – they're extremely rare (about five a year). Many more people are killed globally by elephants and hippos (and, of course, the deadliest creature of all – the mosquito!).

Our brains are basically set up to seek out and hold on to all this bad news. And because we see so much of it and it's so easy to remember, we end up feeling even worse about everything. So, if you feel like the world is a bit of a scary and uncertain place right now, I hear you. Or maybe you think you *should* be feeling like that because the grown-ups around you seem to be worrying and stressed about lots of things. And you wonder if maybe you should be worrying too. It's hard, isn't it?

Now, I'm not saying everything's peachy. There's lots of bad stuff

11

happening, and there is work to be done to make the world a better place.

Of course there is.

But some of that work *is* happening, and there's actually *lots* of good news out there. You just have to find it.

PHEW!

This book is going to put all that good news under the spotlight because we all need happy things to brighten up our day. We all need something to help sort out our worries (or at least take a *few* of them away). And we all need some hope. Hope is so important – if someone figured out how to bottle it up and sell it, they'd be a gazillionaire. We need it to be able to look forward to a positive and exciting future that we are *all* an important part of. I mean, that would be nice, right?

So, let's do this – let's talk about the **GOOD STUFF**. Let's talk about everything from good people in power and good businesses making a difference, to trees healing the planet, robots helping with health care, and amazing everyday people changing the world one step at a time. Let's big these things up so we can feel proud of the world we live in and excited about what might be around the corner if we pull together.

Because you know what?

I BELIEVE IN US.

And, after reading this book, I hope you will too. Just one thing before we kick off: if we're going to be talking about the news – good or bad – there is a *very* important thing we need to talk about first and that's FAKE NEWS.

A YOUNG DETECTIVE'S SUPER-QUICK AND HIGHLY USEFUL GUIDE TO INVESTIGATING

FAKE NEWS

You may have heard of this thing called FAKE NEWS. Well, it's something that is a big problem, but if you get your detective hat on, you can get to the bottom of it.

Here's your super-quick but highly useful guide to understanding what it is and how to bust it.

> FAKE NEWS is news that isn't true. It's *false* or *misleading*.

There are two main types of fake news:

DISINFORMATION: Stories that are deliberately made up to deceive others (to trick people into believing something).

MISINFORMATION: False stories that are shared without deliberately trying to trick people.

A story might start out as *disinformation* then become *misinformation* further down the line. For example, if you steal a cookie but tell everyone that someone else did it, that's *disinformation*. If someone hears that and, without knowing that it's a lie, starts telling everyone that *that* person stole the cookie, that's *misinformation*.

There are also genuine *mistakes*. Maybe the person writing the news hasn't checked all the facts. **UH-OH!** Maybe they were in a rush to get the story out (the news business is intense, after all). Usually, when the facts come to light, reporters who make mistakes will correct their articles with an update. It's very different to the deliberately false stuff! *That's* the stuff you have got to watch out for.

FAKE NEWS THAT ISN'T FAKE

Confusingly, sometimes some people call a story 'fake news' even when it's true. That might be because they don't *want* it to be true or because they don't want *you* to believe it's true! This makes it hard to know *what* to believe. But sometimes you can spot when this is happening because you'll hear the accusation that something's 'fake news' without any concrete evidence to back it up. Evidence, my friend, is key.

> *'I DIDN'T STEAL THE COOKIE! FAKE NEWS! DON'T LISTEN TO THEM BECAUSE ... UMM ... IT'S FAKE NEWS!'*

FAKE NEWS IS NOTHING NEW

Fake news has been around for a long, long time. In ancient times, kings, warriors and soldiers often tricked the enemy into thinking they had huge armies and lots of scary weapons so the enemy wouldn't attack their kingdom. They also used it to turn people against the enemy and mislead them into believing '*their* side' was the best and doing the right thing. In ancient Rome, after the death of Julius Caesar, his adopted son Octavian spread fake news to try and ruin the reputation of Caesar's general, Mark Antony. He even had anti-Antony slogans written on coins! You'll see fake news pop up during wartime, too. It's a sneaky tool politicians use to try and get people on their side. When it's used like this, we call it *propaganda*.

THIS STUFF MOVES *FAST*

The big problem with fake news now is how fast it can travel. A long time ago, before the Internet, TV, radio and printers, it could take

ages for people to find things out. To make the news travel faster, you needed a town crier (a person with a very loud voice!), a carrier pigeon or a messenger on horseback. Then, in the 1440s, a version of the printing press was invented – a machine that made it possible to mass-make books, leaflets, newspapers and posters. (Before this, things were mostly written by hand, one by one! Achy hands all round and, as you can imagine, it took forever.) The printing press meant the news could go much further, much faster. But *now*, with the Internet, all it takes is the click of a button!

CLICK! SEND SHARE

LIKE! GUESS WHAT!!!

You probably know people who use social media so you know just how fast a video or a photograph can **WHOOSH** around the world, and how quickly it can go viral. The same thing can happen with a news story. But WHY would a news story get shared like that? Lots of reasons. Maybe it's interesting or about someone interesting (like a celebrity). Maybe it makes us laugh. Maybe it's surprising or even shocking. Maybe it's a properly juicy bit of gossip. Who can resist sharing that? The thing about fake news is that it tends to tick at least one of those boxes. So it's almost *guaranteed* a trip around the world.

For example, **MAYA** tells **CARLOS** – **CARLOS** shares with all his friends including **AKIKO** – **AKIKO** shares with all *her* friends including **NOAH** ... and so it continues.

CLICKBAIT

Clickbait is a headline or piece of text online that is so exciting or interesting or outrageous that it practically *screams*

'CLICK ME', 'READ ME', 'TELL EVERYONE ABOUT ME!'

People sometimes react to these articles and even share them *before* they've actually read them! News companies love this. With online articles, their job is to make you click.

FRUIT IS ACTUALLY BAD FOR YOU.

*No, it's **NOT**. Don't worry, detectives. That's only if you eat WAYYY too much of it.*

THE SHOCKING TRUTH ABOUT YOUR FAVOURITE MOVIE STARS ... [Dun dun DUNNN ...]

Why? Because they get money from advertisers who pay to have their products advertised next to the news article. Juicy online stories with clickbaity headlines and captions make money by getting lots of clicks and shares.

IS THERE AN ECHO IN HERE?!
ECHO IN HERE?!
ECHO IN HERE?!

There's another ingredient to add to the mix that helps stories spread even faster and that's **CONFIRMATION BIAS.** Sounds very technical, but all it means is that we tend to look for stuff we already agree with and ignore the stuff we disagree with. So, if an article pops up that someone agrees with, they're more likely to share it and talk about it. (There are people out there who believe that humans never landed on the moon – that it was all a big scam (sorry, Neil Armstrong and Buzz Aldrin!). If they see an article that backs that up, you BET they're going to share it. Maybe even before they *read* it!)

Now, because our friends often *tend* to think a bit (or a lot) like us, we end up seeing more and more of the same stuff. It's an:

ECHO CHAMBER ... ECHO CHAMBER ...

The danger is that you can end up in a bubble where you keep hearing and seeing the same messages about the world. You might feel protected in your bubble, but it's actually really important to hear other people's views. To challenge what you think and believe. To learn new things. **EVEN** if it's a piece of news that fits in with what you believe. **EVEN** if it's shared by the cleverest and most honest person you know.

Who knows – it might have been shared in a rush. After all, one BIG challenge we all face today is this ...

INFORMATION OVERLOAD!!!

There is a lot of information out there, and it is being chucked at us with incredible speed. Add in fake news and we've got a serious problem. The news is supposed to be helpful, but when there's so much of it and when some of it is fake, it can get confusing, upsetting and stressful. And with so many people believing and sharing things that just aren't true, it can even be *dangerous.* We need to be able to filter things and sort fact from fiction. It's hard but it IS possible.

TIME TO TURN ON YOUR FAKE NEWS RADAR, DETECTIVES

First of all, STOP. Think. Question *everything.* Not because it's a big bad world and you can't trust anyone. But because you're a detective, and every fine detective knows it's a good habit to *sense-check* the information you take in. Wondering how to do that? Ask these questions, and you'll be sniffing out fake news in no time:

- HANG ON. WHO WROTE THIS, ANYWAY? Check the SOURCE. That's where the story comes from. Where did you find it? On the radio? A newspaper? Is this journalism or is it an advert?

What does this person or organisation believe? What are their values? On websites, look up the 'About Us' section. It might tell you why their stories try to push you in a certain direction.

- **WHO PUBLISHED THE STORY?** Can you trust them? There will (hopefully!) be some well-known news companies or official organisations in your country that are considered trustworthy. There are also some specifically designed for young readers. On the flip side, there will be some that are known for ... err ... *STRETCHING* the truth. Maybe this is something you can chat to a grown-up about. Someone like a parent, a teacher or a librarian – librarians know lots about finding the best sources of information.

GOOD DETECTIVES ARE NEVER TOO SHY TO TALK TO THE EXPERTS.

- **HOW DOES IT MAKE YOU FEEL?** What do you think the person writing it wants you to feel or believe? Fake news stories often get people REALLY worked up. If a story looks like it's trying to do that, whip out your magnifying glass and give it an extra good look.

- **DID YOU CHECK THE DATE?** *Always* check the date. Old stories are sometimes recycled and they can be really misleading.

- **DID THEY BRING IN THE TOP DOGS? THE EXPERTS?** Does the story quote official sources of info such as government sources, the World Health Organisation or the United Nations? Fake news usually won't. It's usually more opinion-flavoured than fact-flavoured.

- **CAN YOU FACT CHECK IT?** Can you find the same story on a really reputable website? (On three websites to be sure.) You can use humans to fact check too if you happen to know someone who knows a great deal about a subject.

- **HEY, HAS SOMEONE BEEN MESSING ABOUT WITH THOSE PHOTOS?** You might be able to spot a fake photo, but not always. Technology is so advanced now that it's possible to create fake photos or videos of people that look very real. But you can often spot something that isn't quite right. It's magnifying-glass-o'clock.

- **IS THERE SOMETHING FISHY ABOUT THIS WEBSITE?** Check for an official website address (URL) such as .gov and .ac or something normal such as .com (but remember, anyone can buy a .com). And look out for mistakes in spelling and grammar – journalists on reputable news sites will *quadruple*-check this sort of thing. Capital letters, bold or underlined text and exclamation marks can be a giveaway too because REPUTABLE NEWS SOURCES DON'T USE CAPITAL LETTERS, **BOLD TEXT**, <u>UNDERLINING</u> AND EXCLAMATION MARKS TO MAKE A POINT!!!!!!!!!!!!!!!

- **IS THIS SOME KIND OF A JOKE?** No, really. There is a chance the story is *supposed* to be poking fun at things (such as an article from *The Onion* or *The Daily Mash* or a magazine such as *Private Eye*).

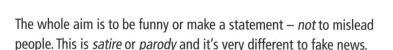

The whole aim is to be funny or make a statement – *not* to mislead people. This is *satire* or *parody* and it's very different to fake news.

But sometimes this can go wrong. That's what happened with The Great Moon Hoax. In 1835, the *New York Sun* printed a bunch of articles about life on the moon (with pictures and everything!). It had things like mini-zebras, unicorns and people with bat-wings. This was intended to be a satire, but the general public actually believed it! This made-up story was hugely popular and was reprinted around the world.

• **FINALLY, WHAT DOES YOUR GUT SAY?** Does the headline and story sound and feel believable? If it's really shocking or outrageous, it might not be true.

That last one's important. You've got your gut. If a story stinks ... it's *probably* fake. At the very least, it's a call to **STOP** and **THINK** and look up multiple alternative trustworthy sources.

GOT ALL THAT?

I know it might feel like a lot to think about, but you don't have to do it all by yourself. When you see a piece of news that raises your eyebrows, it's always worth having a chat with friends, family or teachers. Detectives don't work alone, you know. Putting your heads together is usually a good way to get to the bottom of things! And when you start sniffing out fake news, you'll get better and better at it. There may still be the odd piece that catches you off guard (it happens to all of us!) but your **FAKE NEWS RADAR** should otherwise be pretty solid.

Basically, what I'm saying is ... don't let this overwhelm you. You can still read and watch the news and learn about the world. **YOU JUST HAVE TO STAY SWITCHED ON.**

CHAPTER 1

GOOD HUMANS

A BIG DOLLOP OF KINDNESS, EMPATHY AND HOPE

Before we can be hopeful about the world we live in, we have to be hopeful about that world's busiest, most widespread and most *troublesome* occupants. And that's us. **THE HUMANS.**

Humans do some *terrible* things. No animal has wreaked the kind of havoc we have on this planet and caused the level of environmental damage that we have.

SAD BUT TRUE.

Now, you might be thinking this is *no* way to start a chapter in a book about good news. And if you're now wondering whether we're all truly evil at heart, you're not alone. Great thinkers and philosophers have debated this for thousands of years and no one has really figured it out yet. But the thing is, we don't need humans to be 100 per cent good (phew!). We just need a chink of light and some **HOPE**. Because if there's *enough* goodness in us and if there's enough that's good *about* us, then we should be all right. And hey, here's the **GOOD NEWS** – I really think there is! If anyone tries to tell you otherwise, then here's the ammunition you need to win *that* argument.

#1 VERY COOL HAPPY FACT ABOUT HUMANS: WE'VE GOT EMPATHY

Humans actually do like other humans most of the time. (Aww.) We're born to be social and we've survived as a species because we work together. When our ancestors were hunter-gatherers, working in groups gave us a better chance of finding food and staying safe from scary predators. We're practically *coded* to **CONNECT** to people and look after each other. *Empathy* is one of those important bits of code.

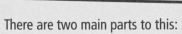

There are two main parts to this:

1. WE'RE SUPER-FEELY. We don't just feel *for* people – we feel *with* them. You know how sometimes you're watching a film and someone's really upset? Watching them, have you ever noticed that you start to feel something too? If you see someone stub their toe – **YOWCH!** – just the thought of it can make you feel something. It's not as painful as stubbing your own toe, but it's some kind of cringy, stingy feeling. Studies show that when we see someone in pain, the same parts of our brain fire off as if we were in pain too!

2. WE CAN PUT OURSELVES IN SOMEONE ELSE'S SHOES. Turns out we are very good at seeing things from a different *perspective*. We can get better at it too by reading books and watching films – anything that helps us learn more about how other people feel and how they see the world. We can **RELATE** to people even if they're very different from us. And that's true whether we're talking about a character in a book or a new neighbour.

All this matters because empathy helps us understand people, what they're feeling and what they really *need*. Once you've got that, it's just one tiny step further to want to help them. And one more step to actually do it! This is where empathy becomes an act of compassion or *kindness*.

GOOD NEWS FLASH!

Kind locals in Mathura, a village in India, have knitted colourful super-size jumpers to keep elephants in a conservation centre warm as temperatures at night plunge to near-zero. Now the elephants can keep cosy and look quite stylish too!

#2 VERY COOL HAPPY FACT ABOUT HUMANS: WE'RE KIND

The news often shows the worst of us humans, so our news-watching alien friend would be forgiven for thinking we're complete **MONSTERS**. But we're not. Not all of the time, anyway. We're actually quite kind.

DON'T LAUGH! IT'S TRUE!

Some of those acts of kindness are little things ...

- sharing
- smiling at a stranger
- helping people carry things if they're struggling
- giving up your seat to someone
- picking up litter
- donating toys or old clothes
- sending a letter or card to someone who is lonely
- giving someone a compliment.

CHALLENGE You probably do these sorts of things all the time without even thinking, but why not try to do at least one act of kindness a day, for an entire week, and watch how happy it can make people. Remember to think about what kind acts people really *need* and will appreciate.

> ## 'TODAY WE SHOULD ALL ASK OURSELVES: WHAT HAVE I DONE TO IMPROVE THE SURROUNDINGS IN WHICH I LIVE?'
>
> **Nelson Mandela**, South African activist and former President

Tragedy and crisis often bring out the best in us, too. Studies have shown that whenever there have been disasters such as earthquakes and floods or acts of terrorism, bystanders have often rushed in to rescue or protect others. And afterwards, people have pulled together to help out and lift up each other's spirits. They have volunteered to give out food parcels, help clean up and provide shelter for those who need it.

Just like everyone else in the world, you'll remember the start of the global COVID-19 pandemic – no matter how surreal, scary and uncertain everything was, people came together. Children put rainbows, hearts and messages of hope in their windows. In Wuhan, China, people chanted *'Jiāyóu!'* from their high-rise apartments (it literally means 'add oil', but it's a way of saying 'keep going' or 'you can do it!'). In Italy, people sang and played music together from their balconies. Everywhere, people checked in on neighbours who were elderly, unwell or vulnerable and needed help getting their food supplies. Companies chipped in too, donating money and switching production lines in their factories to make useful things. Clothing companies such as Gap and car companies such as Aston Martin, for example, started using their factories to make face masks, medical visors and gowns for health care workers. There was this feeling that we're all in this together.

In England, Captain Tom Moore, a 99-year-old war veteran, raised over £32 million for the National Health Service by walking 100 lengths of his garden for his 100th birthday with the help of his walking frame! He was knighted by the Queen and became Captain Sir Tom Moore.

In the USA, ten-year-old Mateo Solis used his birthday money to print flyers for a fundraiser. He raised over $1,000 for a three-year-old girl in hospital with COVID-19.

When the news focuses on the relatively few people who are fighting over toilet rolls, it's easy to forget there's so much kindness out there too. But it *is* out there and we don't have to look too far to find it.

#3 VERY COOL HAPPY FACT ABOUT HUMANS: WE'RE CREATIVE

If empathy and kindness are two reasons we've survived as a species, creativity is another. We're really good at using our imagination to come up with new ideas, solve problems and create things.

Cats can't start a fire to keep themselves warm, build their own houses, play music or dance. But *we* can! Over years and years of human advancement, we've made some amazing things happen. We've even built boxes of wood and metal that can zoom across land and water and some that can carry us to the Moon.

If we wind back hundreds of thousands of years, really early humans couldn't even speak the way we do today. Some scientists believe that at some point around 50,000 to 70,000 years ago, our language got quite sophisticated. Suddenly, early humans could tell other humans some *very* interesting things. Not just about that thing they saw or the danger they swerved – they could even talk about things that *hadn't happened yet.* They could talk about *ideas.*

'MIAAAOW?'

Humans aren't the only creative creatures out there – check out orangutans with their leafy homemade umbrella-hats and back-scratching tools. And bowerbirds, who make 3-D art with things such as acorns, moss, fruit and flowers. But anthropologists (people who study humankind) believe we humans might be the only ones to group our ideas and actually build on them over time.

That means that if one person makes something, another person can add to it or tweak it to make it even better. Or borrow the idea and use it for something completely different.

Did you know that the Slinky was originally designed to secure equipment on ships? And Play-Doh was originally invented to clean wallpaper! Even things like cars have changed over time. Someone came up with the design for a motorcar. It then evolved into better, zippier cars, and now *cleaner* cars such as electric cars that are much better for the environment. It's all one thing building on another!

We are also brilliant at solving problems with very limited resources. JUGAAD in India, GAMBIARRA in Brazil, and JUA KALI in Kenya are Hindi, Portuguese and Swahili words used to describe a quick fix or a 'hack'. It's about thinking *sideways* ...

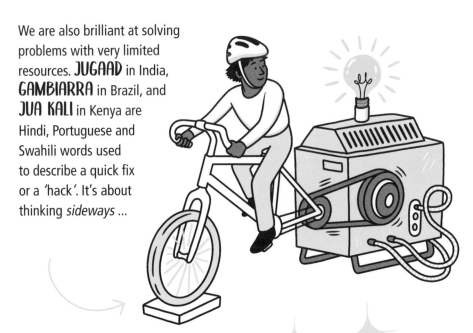

- like an electricity generator that's powered by a bicycle
- a fridge made out of clay
- or a bucket or bottle with holes that turns a tap into a shower (you want to try this one, don't you?).

I'VE GOT TO BE HONEST – these quick fixes may not last long and some people worry about cutting corners. But they're still worth a ton of appreciation as incredible examples of human creativity.

OK, so this is all very cool, but why does it matter? Well ... for lots of reasons. As you know, we're facing a lot of challenges on this planet of ours. And here's the thing – creativity **LOVES** a challenge. This is where it gets to shine.

WHEN THINGS GET TOUGH ✓

... AND WE'RE WORKING WITH LIMITED RESOURCES SUCH AS MONEY OR TIME ✓ ✓

... AND EVERYTHING LOOKS A BIT BLEAK ✓ ✓ ✓

... WE NEED A BREAKTHROUGH.

ENTER CREATIVITY! Throw in a big splash of creativity and we end up with inventions, solutions and new ways of doing things. Such as the wooden handwashing machine put together by nine-year-old Stephen Wamukota in Kenya. A foot pedal makes the water tip and the soap squirt so there's no need to touch the yucky germy taps.

Creativity is also the thing that lets humans harness the power of the wind and sun, develop vaccines and find ways to recycle materials we used to struggle to get rid of.

Creative thinking means we can do the best we can with what we've got (and we don't always have a lot). We'll encounter challenges, but we'll also find ways through them. It's what we do.

CHALLENGE How would **YOU** put your creativity to the test for the greater good? What would you invent to help people? Just imagine. Maybe that's something you'll do in the future – spend your life thinking up creative solutions to the world's biggest problems. How amazing would that be?

#4 VERY COOL HAPPY FACT ABOUT HUMANS: WE CAN LEARN FROM OUR MISTAKES

We humans don't get things right all the time. But we can learn from our mistakes. If we put our hand on something hot – **YOWCH!** – we know not to do *that* again. Being able to learn and change is why many of us have reduced our use of single-use plastics or the amount of water we use in the shower. It's also why we've fought for even bigger changes such as everyone's right to be free, to vote or to be treated fairly, no matter who we are and where we come from. Some *supremely* dodgy things that humans thought were perfectly OK for thousands of years (such as *slavery!*) are now considered shockingly awful and are widely condemned.

We grow, we change. It's part of being human and thank goodness for that. I mean, just imagine what would happen if we *never* learnt from our mistakes!

ACTUALLY, DON'T. THAT'S JUST SCARY!

#5 VERY COOL HAPPY FACT ABOUT HUMANS: WE HAVE HOPE

Hope is one of the best things about us. Now, it might sound like I'm taking you round in circles here – *a big reason to be hopeful about humans is that we are hopeful.*

BUT WAIT. HEAR ME OUT.

What I mean is that we can often see a glimmer of light in all the darkness. We believe things can be better. We dream. When life gets tricky, hope is the thing that lets us see the bright side or better days ahead. When the news is telling us we're **DOOMED**, hope is the little voice that says, 'It's going to be OK.'

Some people are more hopeful than others, sure, and of course there are times when many of us struggle to find that chink of light. But it's so important that there are lots of mental health charities and support groups out there to help people who feel like they've lost hope – such as Mind in the UK and StrongMinds in Uganda and Zambia. Sometimes, we can even give hope to others ourselves – by being there for them, listening and lifting them up when they're down.

Hope is the first step to coming up with all of those wonderfully kind and creative ideas that will make a difference in the world. Without hope, there'd be no point even *trying* to solve a problem. You'd be better off slumping into your sofa and doing nothing.

'... HISTORY HAS SHOWN US THAT COURAGE CAN BE CONTAGIOUS AND HOPE CAN TAKE ON A LIFE OF ITS OWN.'

MICHELLE OBAMA, lawyer, activist and former First Lady of the USA

WHAT'S LEFT TO DO

All right – so we're pretty sure that, overall, people are good at heart – phew! – but we all need to work together so that every day we are:

- empathetic
- kind
- creative
- understanding.

These are the ingredients that can make some amazing things happen – from little everyday changes to the humungous ones.

The world can be scary and humans can be bad *sometimes*, but if enough of us are empathetic, kind, and creative … if enough of us can *learn from our mistakes* and if enough of us have hope … then, you know what?

WE'LL BE OK!

HOW WE GET THERE – WHAT YOU CAN DO

READ UP: Feeling like everyone is just awful and there's no hope? There are pieces of good news everywhere, you just have to know where to find them. With a grown-up, look them up. Find stories about good people and organisations. Read lots of books about true and amazing stories from all over the world – stories of people overcoming challenging times, working together and following their dreams. The more you read the good stuff, the more you realise just how great humans can be. And when you read lots (whether that's true stories or made-up ones), you triple-boost your empathy skills.

KEEP TALKING: On a very small level, you can help bring out the best in people. You can support them and encourage them when they are kind and do nice things. And in a world that likes to talk about the juicy **BAD** stuff, you can talk more about the **GOOD**. Spread it about.

SPEAK OUT: You can also call someone out (gently, but firmly) if the things they're doing are not OK. It might just help them stop and turn things around.

MAKE A CHANGE: Be kind and be creative. Take tiny steps to do some good in the world and lift up the people around you. It doesn't even matter how tiny – a smile, a compliment, just listening to someone (*listening* is underrated). That one kind thing might make all the difference. And you might inspire others to do the same – like a pebble making ripples in a lake. You can also keep reminding yourself that there are a lot of good people out there, even if it might not seem like it. And that people *can* learn from mistakes, and we *can* and *do* change.

CHAPTER 2

GOOD POLITICS

TRAILBLAZERS, DREAM TEAMS AND A BETTER FUTURE

You know when you want to stay up late but the grown-ups say you can't? Or when two people are chatting in class about something *really* important, like what's for lunch today, and the teacher tells them they have to be quiet and listen and maybe even do some work? Well, they can do that because they've got the **POWER**. Politics is all about power. It's about who has it and how they use it. Who gets to make the decisions? Who runs the place? In your house, it'll be a grown-up or a set of grown-ups (though if there's a baby in the house, at times it might feel like it's the baby). In class, it's the teacher. For the whole school, it's the head teacher. You might even have governors and student committees that get to make some decisions too. But most of the time, when grown-ups talk about 'politics' they're not talking about that. They're usually talking about **BIG PICTURE** politics.

ZOOM OUT and you can see who has power when it comes to the whole country. What you call them will depend on where you are in the world. For example, they may be a Prime Minister, President or Chancellor. But this is the Top Dog.

ZOOM IN and you can see who's got power at a local level. These are your local politicians – you might have seen them on the telly with their suits and dodgy haircuts, waffling on about boring stuff. (OK, not all of them – some of them have *awesome* haircuts.)

ZOOM RIGHT IN and you see *us*, the people. We might be the little guys but in lots of political systems, we're supposed to have a lot of power. We'll come back to that on page 45.

So usually how this works is that you have different parties – no, not fun parties with jelly and ice cream, *political* parties – they're

like teams where each party has a leader and lots of less powerful politicians who help them. All parties are meant to work together for the good of the country, but they often compete with each other too, especially during an election when they're all up for the number-one spot.

VOTE FOR US!
WE'RE REALLY
COOL.

VOTE FOR US!
WE'RE EVEN
COOLER.

The party that wins the election becomes the government. They're the people in power and their party leader is the Top Dog. Basically, *they're* the ones who get to make the big decisions.

POLITICAL GRUMBLES

Politics is something you might hear grown-ups grumbling about a lot. That's sometimes because politicians are trying to balance everyone's interests and keep as many people as possible happy. This is hard because all those people can have *very* different ideas about what matters and how to do things!

* 'I was BORN here! I should get special treatment!'
* 'We need people from other countries. We don't have enough teachers, nurses and doctors.'
* 'We need more money for schools!'
* 'What about my small business?'
* 'What about the PLANET?!'

But sometimes grown-ups grumble about how *awful* politicians are. The fact is, they're not totally wrong. There are lots of politicians who use their power selfishly and treat people terribly. You see, power can make people do bad things if they get carried away. They can end up trying to use that power to benefit themselves and their buddies instead of using it for the good of the people. When this happens, it's called:

CORRUPTION.

I'm not going to tell you that stuff isn't true. This book isn't about painting rainbows over all the scary bits. But I *am* going to shine a light on the good things that are happening and the good people doing them. You'll meet some amazing **TRAILBLAZERS** shaking up politics. You'll see some incredible **ACTIVISTS** that have changed things for the better. And you'll visit some pretty cool **INSTITUTIONS** that might even save the world. Right, let's look at the good stuff …

So, we started off by talking about *who has power.* In a 'democracy' – it's you. Us. **THE PEOPLE**.

And guess what?

MORE PEOPLE LIVE IN DEMOCRACIES TODAY THAN EVER BEFORE

Democra-what? If you're wondering exactly what this is, the word 'democracy' comes from the ancient Greek word *démokraiā* – rule by the people. Back in ancient Greece, they had *direct democracy,* where the people voted on everything directly. So they really did rule.

(Although, back then, 'the people' didn't include women, enslaved people or foreigners, so yeah, not exactly *all* the people!)

That's not quite how it works in democracies today. Instead, when we reach the age we're allowed to vote, we elect representatives who rule *for* us. You might have noticed that every few years, your grown-ups go to a polling booth to place their vote (maybe it's at your school and you get a day off!). They'll be given a piece of paper with a few names on it – these are politicians representing different parties – and they tick the person they want. All the votes are counted and the winner is announced!

YESSSS!

Many people around the world think democracy is a good thing, and that's because democratic systems *should* end up being fairer. Now, not all of the world's democracies are perfect. Lots of them have *huge* problems and many are *hybrids* – authoritarian systems (where one person or a very small group has total power) with a *splash* of democracy. But if more people live in democracies than ever before, that means more people in the world have *some* kind of a say in how their countries are run. So it's a jolly good start!

PEOPLE HAVE BEEN FIGHTING FOR – AND WINNING – THE RIGHT TO VOTE

You'd think voting would be something everyone (over a certain age) can do, but that's not always been the case. In *many* countries around the world, some groups of people such as women and Black and indigenous people have only been given the right to vote fairly recently.

INDIGENOUS PEOPLE are people whose ancestors lived on a land way before modern states and borders were a thing.

They include the Aboriginal and Torres Strait Islander peoples who have lived in what is now Australia for over 60,000 years, whereas European settlers actually only rocked up in 1788.

Or the First Nations, Inuit and Métis peoples who have lived in what is now Canada for over 12,000 years, whereas European settlers only arrived in the 16th century.

These are the *original* inhabitants. So the idea that they have had to fight for the right to vote and make decisions about land they've cared for and lived in sync with for so long is … well, it's pretty astonishing, really.

Amazingly, there are also still some countries where it's really hard for women to vote – some are even threatened at the polls.

I KNOW. NONE OF THIS MAKES ANY SENSE.

But we've made a **LOT** of progress thanks to various campaigns for *universal suffrage,* a fancy way of saying that *everybody* should have the right to vote. New Zealand was the first to get there – way back in 1893. As for the rest of the world … well, it took its time, but it got there! Most countries did, anyway.

Number of countries that allowed **ALL** citizens the right to vote:

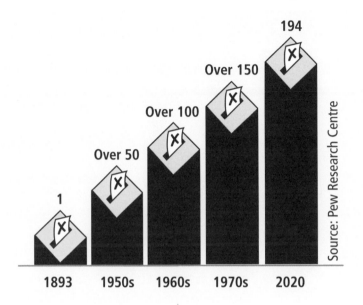

As you can see, that is a **BIG** (and happy!) change in just 120-ish years. People facing injustice for any amount of time is awful, but it doesn't take long to turn things around and make **HUGE** progress.

THERE IS A BIGGER *MIX* OF PEOPLE IN POLITICS THAN EVER BEFORE

Google the greatest politicians in history and you'll get a big old bunch of white men. But look around … that's not really what the world looks like, right? Politicians are supposed to represent all of us. They can do that better if they understand all of us and the different things that affect us and matter to us. And that is easier if there are people on the team who come from lots of different backgrounds too. It's also just a really nice thing to have everyone feel like they can take part in politics. These people become role models for others to look up to and follow in their footsteps.

The good news is, now we are seeing a bigger mix of people in politics:

In **UGANDA**, every political body from the village level right up to parliament has to have reserved seats for disabled politicians. Not everyone thinks reserving seats is the way to go, but here's a country trying to do something good, so let's give them some credit. And because of this policy, Uganda has more disabled politicians than anywhere in the world.

In **AUSTRALIA** in 2016, **LINDA BURNEY**, a Wiradjuri woman, was the first indigenous woman to be voted into the House of Representatives. She's a teacher by training and an indigenous rights activist – a big role model for Aboriginal and Torres Strait Islander peoples and, frankly, for all of us!

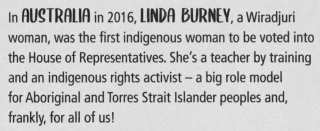

In the **USA**, in 2008, **BARACK OBAMA** became the first Black person to be elected President, something many people didn't think was possible. In 2020, **KAMALA HARRIS,** daughter of an Indian-born mother and Jamaican-born father, became the first woman and the first person of colour to be elected Vice President. She's intelligent, an impressive speaker and a strong leader. In fact, she used to be California's Attorney General, the state's top lawyer and law enforcement officer!

And that's not all. Meet the USA's **ALEXANDRIA OCASIO-CORTEZ** (also known as 'AOC'). AOC is bold and not afraid to challenge things. She's making a lot of noise about the climate emergency and equality. She is of Puerto Rican heritage, was born into a working-class family, worked as a waitress before becoming a politician and is the youngest woman ever to serve in the United States Congress. She's experienced hard times, so she really understands what people are going through and wants to make a difference.

In fact, there are *lots* of impressive women in top positions in politics. Take **JACINDA ARDERN**, Prime Minister of New Zealand from 2017, who showed kind and decisive leadership during a pandemic, a volcanic eruption and a terrorist attack!

We've come a long way. There's still work to do – disabled people, for example, are *massively* underrepresented in politics in most countries – but conversations are happening and change will come. Maybe you will support these politicians too. Maybe one day you will go into politics and properly shake things up! Being a politician is about representing people's interests, and if you go into it for the right reasons, you can really help to create change for the better.

HOW THE NEWS HELPS KEEP DODGY POLITICIANS IN CHECK:

Now, I **KNOW** we did this whole thing earlier on about how negative (or even dangerous!) *some* of the news can be, but reliable, properly fact-checked news is really useful and important. Journalists basically help keep the people in power in check by shining a light on what they're up to. Good journalists will investigate, fact-check things and report back so we all know what's going on **ALL OVER THE WORLD.** Terrible leaders can't just do bad stuff *secretly* any more. Those secrets usually come out in the end!

LOTS OF PEOPLE *CARE* ABOUT POLITICS

You might hear it said that people aren't engaged with politics any more. That they don't vote because they don't see the point. That nobody cares.

ACTUALLY, THEY *DO* CARE.

Look at the 2020 US election. Over 150 million people voted in that election. President Joe Biden got over 80 million votes – more than any other President in American history. In fact, there was a drive to get people registered to vote and some heroes who made that happen. **STACEY ABRAMS**, for example, is a Black lawyer, politician, author, and voting rights activist who helped register over 800,000 voters in Georgia. That's hundreds of thousands of people who now had a chance to have a say in who runs their country. Just **INCREDIBLE**.

And taking part in politics is more than voting. It includes **ACTIVISM** – taking action to change the world. People from very different backgrounds all coming together because they want justice, not just power. If you ever lose faith in politicians or think they need to do better, you can take a leaf out of the Mini-Handbook for Activists and try to bring about change in other ways.

MINI-HANDBOOK FOR ACTIVISTS

GET ON YOUR FEET: Marches and demonstrations have taken place throughout history and around the world. In 1930 in colonial India, Mahatma Gandhi led thousands of Indians on a 380-kilometre Salt March to protest against the British law that Indians couldn't collect or sell salt (yes, salt – it's actually so important. Just try going without it for a week!). In 1969, half a million Americans marched on Washington to protest against the war in Vietnam. More recently people have marched in support of causes such as marriage equality and Black Lives Matter (a movement we'll look at in Chapter 5).

SKIP THOSE SHOPS: *Boycotts* are where people stop buying certain products to put pressure on a company or even a whole country by hitting it where it hurts: their WALLET. From the 1950s to the 1980s, for example, South African activists called on the world to boycott South African products to protest against APARTHEID – a terrible system of racial segregation, which started in 1948 and came to an end in the early 1990s. Boycotting those products was like a big signal to say, 'Listen, we are not cool with what is going on, so stop it.'

WRITE THOSE LETTERS: I'm not saying you should get yourself a political pen pal, but if you write to politicians, sometimes you may find that they'll not only read the letter or email but they'll send a reply too. It's their job to listen to the people they

CLIMATE EMERGENCY

represent and, if they disagree with them, they might take the time to explain why. If local politicians get lots of letters about a cause, they'll take notice and raise it with the politicians the next level up, and so on and so on. A short, punchy, *specific* letter or email can be really powerful.

SIGN THOSE PETITIONS: Petitions are where people gather signatures to support a call for action or change. They're usually part of a bigger campaign with lots of other things going on. Petitions used to be on paper, (sometimes very loooonnnnng rolls of paper!) but now they're online and can be shared and signed in a jiffy.

GET THE WORD OUT: Social media can help messages reach hundreds of thousands of people around the world, like they did in 2011 when Manal al-Sharif, leader of the Women2Drive campaign, posted a video of herself driving in Saudi Arabia when women were not allowed to drive. She was arrested but the rules were eventually changed.

WALK THE WALK (QUIETLY): You don't have to get out there and march or make speeches. *Quiet activism* works too. That means doing little things every single day wherever you can and making a difference *without* telling the whole world about it. It might be things such as sticking up for other people; including them when they're left out; having gentle 1–2–1 conversations to raise awareness about issues; quietly buying from companies that do good; or quietly making decisions to help take care of the planet (such as recycling or upcycling things or growing your own vegetables).

POVERTY, EQUALITY

CHALLENGE Is there a big cause you care about? What could you do about it? Could you use some of the tricks from the Mini-Handbook for Activists?

WHAT IS THE POINT?

Sometimes you might question whether *talking* about big issues is enough. Do people just do it for show – because it's *cool* to support big causes? Because it's *cool* to post these things on social media or to march and come up with clever slogans and pictures for your posters? Will it change anything?

The answer is yes, it CAN. In the long run. It can start a conversation and *that* can turn into action. If more people know and care about an issue, they start doing things like writing to politicians, donating time and money to the cause and (when they can) voting in a way that makes a difference. While social media *can* be dangerous (hello, fake news), it can also be really helpful in getting people organised, bringing them together, and telling the whole world what's happening.

MEET THE ACTIVISTS

There are so many incredible young activists out there – like AUTUMN PELTIER, the Anishinaabe-kwe activist from the Wikwemikong First Nation who has been campaigning for water conservation since she was eight.

Or LESEIN MUTUNKEI, the football-loving environmentalist from Kenya who started Trees 4 Goals when he was 12 years old, encouraging people to plant trees every time they score a goal (his big dream is for FIFA to make it a thing for *world* football).

And **MALALA YOUSAFZAI**, the youngest Nobel Peace Prize winner and an activist for girls' right to an education.

There are almost too many to list here and more popping up every day. That's **GOT** to be a reason to be hopeful!

> 'KEEP GOING, DON'T LOOK BACK, AND IF YOU HAVE AN IDEA, JUST DO IT; NO ONE IS GOING TO WAIT FOR YOU OR TELL YOU WHAT TO DO, USE YOUR VOICE AND SPEAK UP.'
>
> AUTUMN PELTIER, Anishinaabe-kwe water activist

GOOD NEWS FLASH!

In 2016, eight-year-old Mari Copeny wrote a letter to then-President Barack Obama telling him about the contaminated water in Flint, Michigan. The President not only replied to her letter but he travelled to Flint to meet her and to find out more. He later signed off on a $100 million budget to help fix the water system!

TEAMWORK MAKES THE DREAM WORK

In the news we see lots of stories of war and conflict and tensions bubbling away between countries (and sadly, these conflicts do exist, and civil wars, for example, are still happening). But if we zoom out far enough, researchers say the world as a *whole* is experiencing quite an extraordinary time of peace and international cooperation. Because of the news, it's easy to lose sight of the fact that although countries have their issues with each other (huge ones, clearly), they actually often work together on all kinds of big and important projects such as human rights, global health and space exploration.

> THAT'S KIND OF A BIG DEAL.

> 'MORE THAN EVER BEFORE IN HUMAN HISTORY, WE SHARE A COMMON DESTINY. WE CAN MASTER IT ONLY IF WE FACE IT TOGETHER.'
>
> **KOFI ANNAN,** Secretary-General of the UN 1997–2006

THE UNITED NATIONS (THE UN)

We can't talk about countries working together without talking about the UN. Now, if you're thinking that 'the United Nations' sounds like some sort of superhero alliance, you're not far off. The UN was set up in 1945 after the Second World War to help keep things friendly between countries and to get them working together to do good (and superheroey) things such as protecting human rights and solving the world's problems. It's actually 'Take 2'. 'Take 1' was the League of Nations, which was set up in 1919 after the First World War and fell apart by the 1940s after it failed to stop *another* world war from breaking out. Yep – *total* disaster for a peacekeeping body.

The UN was designed to be more powerful and more effective, and it involved way more countries than the League of Nations. As I write this, there are 193 member countries signed up – 193! Whatever people say about the UN, *that* is an incredible achievement. It's amazing that we have so many countries on (mostly) the same page in thinking world peace and protecting human rights sounds like **A VERY GOOD IDEA.**

One of the things the UN has worked on recently is a list of Millennium Development Goals. Things like, you know, eradicating extreme poverty and hunger, making primary education available to everyone everywhere and protecting the environment. That kind of thing. UN members wanted to hit these targets by 2015, and they didn't *quite* make it, but they've taken BIG steps in the right direction, and we'll look at some of those later on in this book. Next stop for

the UN: The 17 Sustainable Development Goals for 2030, which include:

- **NO** poverty
- **ZERO** hunger
- good health and wellbeing for **EVERYONE**.

And a promise: to 'leave no one behind'. It's a big and bold dream but the best dreams usually are, aren't they? If that doesn't fill your heart with a warm fuzzy feeling of hope for the future, I don't know what will!

EXPLORING SPACE

But it's not just about things that are happening on the ground. Governments and countries also work together in … space! Space is expensive to get to and explore and building something as big the International Space Station (the 'ISS') or the Gateway (a new outpost that will orbit the moon) isn't something any one country can easily do alone.

In fact, five space agencies covering 15 nations worked together to build the ISS. Different sections were made by different countries and blasted up into space, where the ISS was assembled while orbiting the Earth at 28,000 kilometres per hour! I mean … **WOW!** The space agencies all brought different skills to the table – such as Canada and Japan with their robotics knowledge and Russia with its Soyuz spacecraft. After the retirement of the US Space Shuttles in 2011 and before the development of SpaceX's Crew Dragon or Boeing's

Starliner, the USA's space agency, NASA, relied on Russian Soyuz spacecraft to launch their astronauts and supplies to and from the ISS. That's quite amazing, actually, because these two nations have historically had *very* frosty relations (you may have heard of the Cold War and the 'Space Race').

Like the ISS, the Gateway will be a space station and laboratory, but it'll also be a sort of spacey pit stop for anyone exploring the Moon and, one day, Mars. A bit like an airport … or spaceport! It's a huge project, and space agencies need to buddy up to make it happen!

GOOD NEWS FLASH!

Story Time From Space. Do you ever look up at the stars before you go to bed? Well you can actually watch astronauts reading bedtimes stories and do science experiments live on the International Space Station! Videos are beamed down to Earth for everyone to enjoy while the astronauts orbit our planet approximately 16 times a day!

TOGETHER'S JUST *BETTER!*

Luckily, as you can see, WORKING TOGETHER is something humans are actually quite good at. Or we *can* be. We see that in politics but also in other areas such as the fight to protect our planet and our health and to get rid of inequality. And we'll be looking at *all* of that in the next few chapters.

WHAT'S LEFT TO DO

- We need more strong, compassionate leaders who are there to represent the people and not just flex that power for personal gain.
- We need more politicians that reflect and represent *everyone* in society.
- We need countries to keep working together. We get a lot more done and make the biggest difference when we do.

HOW WE GET THERE – WHAT *YOU* CAN DO

READ UP Use the news to stay on top of what's happening in the world (but remember all the stuff about watching out for fake news – see page 13.)

KEEP TALKING Chat to your friends and family about the issues that matter to you. They may not always agree with you but by talking *(nicely)*, you can find a middle ground and at least *understand* each other. The trouble with politics is that we surround ourselves with people who think the same as us so we end up in little echo chambers. Remember those? That means we don't get challenged and we don't learn and grow. *Talking is good.*

SPEAK OUT You can be an activist by speaking out and writing to your local politicians when you see something you want to change. You can encourage people to buy things from good companies and swerve the not-so-good ones. And when you're old enough to vote, you can *use that vote* to chuck out the politicians you dislike and bring in the good ones! In the meantime, get the grown-ups *around* you to vote. Some will tell you there's no point, that nothing ever changes. You can tell them every vote counts. As the African proverb goes:

IF YOU THINK YOU'RE TOO SMALL TO MAKE A DIFFERENCE, YOU HAVEN'T SPENT THE NIGHT IN A ROOM WITH A MOSQUITO!

MAKE A CHANGE Who knows? Maybe one day *you'll* be a politician (you might be able to get some practice in today by standing for a role in your school). But whatever you do, you don't need to do it alone. Real change happens when we work together.

CHAPTER 3

GOOD PLANET

SUPERTREES, CLEAN CARS AND A WHOLE LOT OF GREEN GOODNESS

Humans are so small in the grand scheme of things and we haven't actually been here very long as a species, but our footprint on this planet is **HUMUNGOUS**. Thanks to all our activity (chopping down trees, burning fossil fuels such as coal, oil and natural gas, building up waste mountains, that kind of thing), the world faces *many* challenges. Such as these ones here:

- climate change
- deforestation
- the extinction of plants and animals
- air and water pollution
- water shortages.

YEP. IT'S A LOT.

Now, many of these issues are interconnected, but there's one that stands out as *the* issue of our time and that's **CLIMATE CHANGE**. You've probably heard of this already but what it means is that the Earth is heating up. And not in a nice ooh-let's-go-somewhere-warm-and-sunny kind of way. In a dangerous way.

THE GREENHOUSE EFFECT. This effect is what makes Earth warm enough for us to live on. Here's how it works:

Greenhouse gases in our atmosphere such as water vapour, carbon dioxide and methane trap a big chunk of the heat from the Sun and keep our planet nice and cosy.

If this effect is too weak, you get something like **MARS!** *Freeeezing.*

If this effect is *super*-strong, you get something like **VENUS** – its surface is hot enough to melt lead!

If this effect is juuuust right, you get our planet: Earth. Well, Earth before the Industrial Revolution kicked off in the second half of the 18th century! As you can see, a bit of greenhouse effect is a good thing, but too much is a problem. And right now, we're leaning towards too much because things such as burning fossil fuels, driving cars and trucks and cutting down forests all increase the amount of carbon dioxide in our atmosphere.

Our human activity has made the Earth heat up by at least 1°C since the Industrial Revolution. That might not sound like a big deal to you, but it certainly is a big deal to life as we know it! It affects the quality of soil and causes water shortages. It means more (and more intense) extreme weather conditions, causing things like hurricanes, floods, droughts, heatwaves and wildfires – we're already seeing some of these around the world. It means glaciers and ice sheets are melting faster than ever before, which makes sea levels rise. If nothing is done, large parts of cities such as New York City, Rio de Janeiro and Shanghai could be underwater *in our lifetimes.*

'FAKE NEWS!!!' OR IS IT?!

Remember I said that *some* people call things fake news even when they're true? Well, climate change is one of those things. But the science is actually really clear. In the news, you sometimes see one scientist talking about climate change and one who doesn't believe it's caused by human activity. That might make it look like climate experts are split 50/50 on this but they're *not.* The overwhelming majority of them agree that climate change is real and that it's seriously bad news.

Things are bad at 1°C, but scientists say they will be *catastrophic* at 3°C, which is where they think we're headed at the end of the century if we don't do something to stop it. The danger threshold is 1.5°C, and that's the level we're trying to keep it – go beyond that and it's not looking good. We're already seeing how climate change affects people, plants and wildlife, but if things get worse, we could be looking at a mass extinction event unlike anything we've seen since 66 million years ago when non-avian dinosaurs were wiped off the face of the Earth (probably because of a humungous asteroid crashing into it)!

GULP!

And this is supposed to be a *hopeful* book?! YIKES.

> 'I'M OFTEN ASKED WHETHER I BELIEVE IN GLOBAL WARMING. I NOW JUST REPLY WITH THE QUESTION: DO YOU BELIEVE IN GRAVITY?'
>
> **NEIL DEGRASSE TYSON,** American astrophysicist

OK. I know how it looks. But there *are* reasons to be hopeful and we're going to find them. Some people think hope isn't a good idea when it comes to things like climate change. Because hope can make you sit back and relax, cross your fingers and do nothing. But that's not the kind of hope I'm talking about. I mean the hope that makes you believe this is a fight worth fighting. However tired or worried you feel, hope gives you a reason to give this your 100 per cent. That's just what we need to support the people and organisations that are working to protect our planet.

There's good news out there. Like little green shoots. Here's one of them ...

PEOPLE ARE *TALKING* ABOUT THIS STUFF

You can't solve a world problem that nobody knows about. Or one nobody believes is a problem. Yes, frustratingly, there are still some people out there who call it fake news, but more and more people are aware of climate change now (or rather, the climate *emergency*). Ordinary people like you and me see it as a major issue. It's in the news again and again. Activists are speaking out about it. More and more *companies* are talking about it. *Governments* are talking about it.

People are doing something about it too. Millions of people have taken part in protests around the world to put pressure on governments to take action. So far, over 100 countries have promised to reach net-zero carbon emissions by 2050. This will be achieved by:

- A promise to cut emissions down and make sure that any released are balanced by reducing greenhouse gases elsewhere (e.g. by planting trees).
- Switching to cleaner energy such as wind and solar energy, using electric (or hydrogen-powered) cars and trucks, building more walking and cycle routes.
- Making homes ecofriendly.
- Cutting waste right down.
- Restoring nature.

SOME COOL CLIMATE ACTION: We've got organisations such as Rewilding Europe looking at bringing back wildlife and native trees, restoring nature's balance. We've got companies such as Tesla and China's BYD making electric cars to replace our gas guzzlers (more about clean cars on page 84.)

And companies such as Google who are working on running all their data centres and offices on carbon-free energy by 2030. Not only that; we have some very clever people all around the world working on something called *carbon capture technology* – machines that can suck CO_2 right out of the atmosphere! Some scientists believe that it could really help in the fight to drive down emissions.

'HUMAN BEINGS ARE THE MOST ADAPTABLE ORGANISM THAT HAS EVER APPEARED ON THE PLANET AND IS EXTRAORDINARILY RESOURCEFUL AND VERY GOOD AT LOOKING AFTER ITSELF. IF IT TURNS ITS ATTENTIONS TO LOOKING AFTER OTHER THINGS AS WELL, WHICH IT IS EQUALLY GOOD AT, IF IT BOTHERS TO DO SO, THEN THERE IS HOPE.'

SIR DAVID ATTENBOROUGH, naturalist, broadcaster and environmental activist

Sir David Attenborough and Prince William have joined forces to create the Earthshot Prize – a £50 million fund to find 50 creative solutions to the world's BIGGEST environmental problems. It's all about five 'Earthshots' or goals: to protect and restore nature, clean our air, revive our oceans, build a waste-free world and fix our climate. Each year, for ten years, five winners get £1 million each to shake up the world. And anyone can apply – schools, communities, businesses, governments, ANYONE.

HITTING THE RESET BUTTON ON NATURE

People all over the world are trying to solve the mind-boggling problem of how to reduce greenhouse gases quickly, cheaply and safely. But nature has actually already got it all figured out. Trees absorb the carbon dioxide we humans breathe out, and the carbon dioxide we create too. Tropical forests are especially good at this. They lock up those greenhouse gases, for *free*. Amazing, right? The world is incredible and that is something to feel good about.

But the bad news is when we come along with our axes and chop them down! We've already wiped out around half of the world's trees since the start of human civilisation. Now, every year, we cut down around *15 billion* trees – a forest the size of the UK! – to collect wood for timber and to make space to build homes, mine or drill the land, grow things, or graze livestock. Not only do we lose our greenhouse-gas lockers, but *all* these activities create even *more* greenhouse gases! When trees are chopped down and burned, or when they rot, the carbon stored in them is released into the air.

Farming is an issue too. You've got nitrous oxide from fertilisers and methane from burpy livestock (seriously!) and manure (POO!). Drilling and mining can be really bad too, so basically, however you look at it, deforestation is a greenhouse-gas bonanza. And that's before we even get to the terrible impact it has on plants, animals and the people who live in and around those forests!

TURNING THIS SHIP AROUND

Back to the good news. We can turn it around. We've got two options and we need to do both of them:

1. STOP CHOPPIN' DOWN THE TREES (protect the world's forests from deforestation)

2. MAKE THE WORLD GREEN AGAIN (reforestation and rewilding).

You might hear about climate strikers in big cities, and they're doing really important work speaking out about the climate emergency. But indigenous communities around the world have been doing this work since *forever*. Not only speaking out about the world's forests, but *protecting* them too. They're deeply connected to nature and live in balance with it. They see it as something to respect and honour, so they're not out there overfishing, overworking the soil or destroying the forest. Nope. These communities are *in tune* with their surroundings. And they're absolute pros at tracking and monitoring species of plants and animals, just like any other conservation experts.

There are indigenous communities all over the world from Brazil and Ecuador to China, India, Indonesia, and all over the continent of Africa. The land where they live is very different from country to country, but it's bursting with life. The Amazon rainforest, for example, with its thick, bright-green canopies and winding river, is home to 40,000 types of plant, 3,000 types of fish, 430 mammals and 2.5 *million* types of insect. It's **AMAZING.**

If we want to protect our forests, we have to protect the land rights of indigenous people. Nobody understands nature and takes care of it like they can. They make up less than 5 per cent of the world's population, but the land they care for is home to an incredible 80 per cent of the world's **BIODIVERSITY**.

Sadly, despite doing the least to hurt the planet, indigenous communities are often the biggest victims of climate change. And very often they have to fight hard to protect their land. Like in 2019, when after a long legal battle, the people of Indonesia's Aru Islands stopped a plan to turn more than half their land into a *ginormous* sugar plantation. There are battles like this going on all over the world – indigenous people and their allies defending nature with all they've got.

It's important we understand the traditions of indigenous communities and work with them to protect our planet.

'WE HAVE BEEN PROTECTING THE WORLD'S BIODIVERSITY FOR HUNDREDS OF YEARS AND WE WILL KEEP DOING THAT AND WE ARE NOT GOING TO STOP, WE ARE NOT GOING ANYWHERE.'

HELENA GUALINGA, activist from the Sarayaku community in Ecuador

GOOD NEWS FLASH!

New Zealand has passed laws recognising a river (Te Awa Tupua), a rainforest (Te Urewera) and a mountain (Taranaki) as legal persons with individual rights just like ours – like the right to be protected from harm!

Under the law, the Māori people (who see these natural features as their ancestors) are considered their legal guardians together with the government. So, if they're harmed, Māori can take it up in court! And guardians is the perfect word in other ways too. Today, for example, scientists and activists are working with Māori elders to save the old kauri trees from a new and deadly disease called kauri dieback. One ancient fix? Ground-up fat and bones from beached whales that don't survive. It is believed that the whales and the kauri are connected and that the whales come to the shore to help them.

THE GREEN HALL OF FAME

There have been lots of reforestation and rewilding projects undertaken around the world. And people working to make agriculture 'greener' too (because that's another big offender when it comes to greenhouse gases):

COSTA RICA had lost so much of its rainforest to deforestation but it has **GREENED** up. Forest cover has doubled in 30 years and now *half* of its surface is covered in trees, creating a massive carbon sink.

A Great Green Wall of trees is being built across the width of **AFRICA** – 8,000 kilometres of trees running through over 20 countries. Millions of acres of degraded land have been restored already.

A huge urban farm has opened up … on a rooftop in **PARIS**! A London company is doing a similar thing but *underground* in an old air-raid shelter! There are lots of these farms popping up. Imagine. Seasonal fruits and vegetables, grown locally, within a short walk from home. If this takes off worldwide, it'd increase city greenery, cut right down on 'food miles' and do a lot to protect forests.

Speaking of rooftops, **SINGAPORE** has lots of high-rise sky gardens and vertical urban garden structures called *Supertrees*. As well as being packed with beautiful plants such as orchids and climbing vines, they do interesting things such as collecting rainwater or generating solar power.

Countries such as **SWEDEN** and the **USA** have been working on restoring their sea meadows. *(Did you know these were a thing?! I didn't!)* In 2020, 750,000 seagrass seeds were planted just off the coast of Wales in the UK. Turns out seagrass absorbs carbon *35 times* faster than rainforests, and they lock in 10 per cent of the ocean's carbon!

Groups and governments around the world are looking into **REGENERATIVE FARMING** – a fancy term for farming techniques that are in sync with nature rather than being a bit weird and artificial and working against it! Some of that is going back to that ancient indigenous knowledge we talked about. Like in Burkina Faso, a small country in West Africa, where a farmer called Yacouba Sawadogo used a traditional African farming method called zai to turn a huge chunk of abandoned barren land into a lush forest.

CHALLENGE Imagine you are in charge of a brand-new city (CONGRATULATIONS!). How would you make your city super-green? What ideas have you got up your sleeve to tackle the climate emergency?

LOAD UP THE VEGGIES

We've already talked about greenhouse-gas issues with livestock. It makes up about 15 per cent of greenhouse gases. Now *I'm* not here to tell you what to eat and what not to eat, but studies show that if we want to hit our climate-change goals, we humans need to think about *cutting down* on meat and dairy. There are a bunch of things happening to help with that – like Meatless Mondays, more vegan and vegetarian options in restaurants and schools and cleverly designed meat-free and dairy-free alternatives to use at home.

Vienna's Vegetable Orchestra tours the world with its carrot flutes, leek violins, pepper trumpets and pumpkin drums. All the instruments used are made entirely from vegetables and nothing's wasted. Anything left over gets cooked into a yummy soup, which is served up to the audience after the show!

GOOD NEWS FLASH!

CLEANING UP OUR ACT

Guess what? A good chunk of the technology we need to move from *dirty* energy to *clean* energy already exists and is constantly being improved. In two thirds of the world, wind and solar energy are already the *cheapest* types of energy around. That's right – the clean stuff is *cheaper* than the *dirty* stuff. That helps. A lot! And it is getting cheaper and better all the time (and so are batteries to store all that power).

There are different types of clean energy, and we'll need a mix of them if we're going to get away from those pesky fossil fuels (with coal being the *dirtiest* and baddest baddie of them all):

HYDROPOWER
(from moving water)
WIND ENERGY (from the wind)
SOLAR ENERGY (from the sun)
BIOFUEL ENERGY (from plant and animal waste)
GEOTHERMAL ENERGY (from the heat stored deep within the Earth)
GREEN HYDROGEN
(from electrolysed water)

MEET GREEN HYDROGEN – THE NEW KID ON THE BLOCK:

Hydrogen is the most abundant element in the universe but on Earth, it's usually hanging out with another element. Buddied up with oxygen, it makes **WATER.** A big burst of electricity can extract that hydrogen through a process called electrolysis. Power that by wind turbines or solar energy and you've got a fully green form of hydrogen energy! It's an exciting thing some scientists are working on. Some people think it could change the way we heat our homes and run our vehicles, even big ones such as trains, buses and trucks (and, one day, maybe even planes). Or it might be a type of energy to fill the gaps or store away as back-up for some of these other sources. **BUT** it's pricey. And hydrogen is very ... ahem ...

EXPLOSIVE!

It's going to take some work, but is one to watch out for!

It's not all rosy though. You might hear that China (the biggest greenhouse-gas emitter by *far*) is the world's largest investor in clean energy **(YAY!)** but also the world's biggest consumer of ... coal **(BOO!).** And India is doing lots with clean energy but it still uses coal too. But hold on a second. There are a few things you need to know to put that in context ...

These are countries with humungous populations. Together, India and China make up *over a third* of the world's population. That's a *lot* of people to feed and house and look after. So yes, these countries use up a lot of energy. But when you look at their greenhouse gas emissions per person (for the maths lovers out there, that's total emissions in a country divided by the number of people in it!), they're actually *much lower* in China and India than they are in the USA.

And I'm not saying this to let these countries off the hook! They're *still* working on doing better. China has promised to get emissions

down to net zero by 2060 and is splashing the cash on wind and solar. Meanwhile, India, (one of the biggest carbon-emitters after China and the USA) now invests more in solar than coal. And made some pretty bold promises to reduce its carbon footprint.

There's good news on the other side of the world too. In 2019, Costa Rica got a whopping *99 per cent* of its energy from clean sources, with Norway just behind it. And in 2021, Iceland and Paraguay were at 100 per cent, with more and more countries around the world wanting to join the party.

Now, this move from dirty energy to clean energy is like a breath of fresh air, but electricity (and heat) generation makes up around a quarter of the world's greenhouse-gas emissions. Another chunk comes from *transport*. So let's look at that ...

CHANGING HOW WE GET AROUND

Transport is *dirty*. It's got a lot to answer for when it comes to chucking out greenhouse gases, and road vehicles such as cars, buses and trucks are the worst offenders. In countries such as the UK and the USA this is even more of an issue than electricity generation.

VROOM VROOOOOM

But things are changing.

Because now we've got ELECTRIC vehicles.

They're cleaner and greener and sales are growing around the world. So is the choice on offer, and batteries are getting more powerful so the cars can go further on a single charge. These cars are becoming more affordable too, and we're starting to see more and more charging points across cities, which makes going electric a whole lot easier!

One study reckons that by 2050, every second car on the streets all around the world could be an electric car. That'd cut carbon emissions by about as much as all the current emissions of *Russia*.

There are also *hybrid* cars that can run on petrol/diesel *and* electricity – like a little in-betweeny option while we transition to clean cars. The longer they're run on electricity, the lower the emissions.

And it's not just cars. We're talking:

- electric two- and three-wheelers
- electric buses
- electric vans and trucks
- even heavy-duty trucks (the real monsters of the road) are slowly going electric.

These things will take time, but some countries are giving it a big push. Some have even set a date to ban the sale of new cars with combustion engines (basically the fossil-fuel burners). Cities such as London, Barcelona and Beijing have introduced special low-emission zones, banning cars that chuck out too many emissions (there are over 250 zones like this in Europe alone!).

And what about cars powered by a (green) hydrogen fuel cell? The only waste they emit is *water vapour!* There aren't too many around just yet but they could take off in the future. Some people think electric is still the way to go for cars, but hydrogen fuel cells might help with bigger vehicles such as buses and trucks. And these new technologies are getting more efficient all the time! Either way, the future is bright and very green.

HANG ON. GET OUT OF THE CAR! It's not just about building cleaner cars and buses and trucks. It's also about cutting down on how much we use them – walking or cycling or jumping on to public transport wherever possible (and it isn't possible for *everyone*). Here are some cities that deserve LOTS of gold stickers on this front:

COPENHAGEN: A city where cycling rules! It's the main form of transport (there are more bikes than cars!), and the whole place is very walkable.

LONDON: It's got a growing fleet of electric taxis and buses, a big rail and underground train network and famous bike rental services.

PARIS: It's got around *1,000 km* of bike lanes, and it's a city where a major riverside highway has been converted into a pedestrian promenade.

HONG KONG: It's got a cheap and super-efficient public transport system (especially its metro!), which handles over 90 per cent of daily journeys in the city. That's a lot.

SÃO PAULO: This big city is making a big shift from cars to cleaner ways to travel. It's one to watch! Got to get marks for improvement too, right?

See? There's lots happening on all these fronts. More than I can cram into this chapter. It's going to take a pick and mix of approaches to tackle the climate emergency, but there's hope. There really is.

'I DO HAVE REASONS FOR HOPE: OUR CLEVER BRAINS, THE RESILIENCE OF NATURE, THE INDOMITABLE HUMAN SPIRIT AND ABOVE ALL, THE COMMITMENT OF YOUNG PEOPLE WHEN THEY'RE EMPOWERED TO TAKE ACTION.'

DR JANE GOODALL, primatologist and conservationist

WHAT'S LEFT TO DO

- Stop wiping out our forests, especially our tropical forests. Seriously. STOP IT.
- Greenify the world with reforestation and rewilding projects and regenerative agriculture.
- Protect the land rights of indigenous people – they *know* how to take care of nature.
- Replace fossil fuels with clean energy everywhere, from how we travel to how we light up and heat up the world.
- Redesign cities so they're super-friendly for people walking and cycling and with nice big, affordable and reliable public transport networks.

HOW WE GET THERE – WHAT YOU CAN DO

READ UP: Get to know the big issues (and watch out for fake news again!). Find out what different companies and countries are doing to make a difference.

KEEP TALKING: ... about the climate emergency. Use your voice to spread the word and *especially* to lift up indigenous and local voices whose stories can sometimes get lost.

SPEAK OUT: Write letters to your local politicians if they're not doing enough and need a gentle nudge (or a big one). Write to the CEOs (the big cheeses) at companies too. Ask them to do better.

MAKE A CHANGE: Support companies that are doing their bit to help with the climate emergency (and think about avoiding the ones that aren't, or reach out to them to see if they'll change their ways). Use public transport wherever you can or whip out your bike or walking shoes (if possible). You totally do this already, I'm sure, but switch off those electrical devices when you're not using them to save on electricity, and see if the grown-ups can change light bulbs for energy-saving ones too. Cut down on *waste* – whether that's the stuff you wear (and chuck away) or the food you eat. And speaking of food, go for seasonal, locally grown goodies wherever possible and remember to load up on those veggies!

CHAPTER 4

GOOD HEALTH

HEALTH HEROES, ROBOTS AND FUNKY TOILETS

You might have seen health zoom into the spotlight recently with the COVID-19 pandemic. We've seen lots of people worrying about health and wanting to protect it, but what do *you* think it means to be healthy? It's not about neatly fitting into a box with a fixed image of what a 'healthy' person *looks* like. We're all different, aren't we? But there are some things that we'd all agree on and that's a list of a few essentials we all need to keep us going. We all need clean water – to drink, to wash, to cook. We all need toilets of some kind and ones that safely get rid of all the ... err ... 'waste'! If we don't have those things (and a clean place to live), we can end up with all sorts of diseases that *could* have been avoided. Oh, and we need access to health care too – to help us prevent some of those diseases, to find out if we have them, and to help sort things out if we do!

SOUNDS LIKE A REALLY BASIC LIST, RIGHT?
CAN'T BE THAT HARD, CAN IT?

BUT, ACCORDING TO THE WORLD HEALTH
ORGANISATION, BILLIONS OF PEOPLE
AROUND THE WORLD DON'T HAVE ALL
THOSE THINGS ...

AROUND **1/2** THE WORLD'S POPULATION STILL **DOESN'T** HAVE ACCESS TO ESSENTIAL HEALTH CARE.

1 IN EVERY 10 PEOPLE ON THE PLANET DON'T EVEN HAVE ACCESS TO BASIC DRINKING WATER.

OVER FOUR BILLION PEOPLE DON'T HAVE ACCESS TO SAFELY MANAGED SANITATION

(SOME KIND OF HOME TOILET SYSTEM THAT TAKES CARE OF THE WASTE).

THAT'S OVER HALF THE WORLD'S POPULATION.

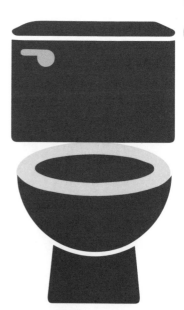

And the biggest issue? The gap between the people that have this stuff and the ones that don't is **HUUUUGE.** Some countries are doing OK but for some, the situation's just awful. So, it's not really that surprising that headlines about global health are some of the scariest ones out there!

But you know where to go for the bad news. This book is about the *good* news. As always, there are people and companies and charities and *whole governments* on the case. And though you might have to look a bit harder to find them, there are things that are improving too. Improvements aren't catchy headline material but they mean a lot. Every improvement is a life saved or made better in some way. Sometimes millions of lives.

> ## 'HOW WONDERFUL IT IS THAT NOBODY NEED WAIT A SINGLE MOMENT BEFORE STARTING TO IMPROVE THE WORLD.'
>
> **ANNE FRANK,** German-born Jewish Second World War diarist

FIGHTING DISEASE: SUCCESS STORIES

VACCINES AND THE ANTIBODY DOJO

Speaking of *improvements* that save millions of lives – vaccines for preventable diseases are right up there (but keep an eye out – there's also a lot of fake news about vaccines and it spreads so fast it makes some people hesitant to take them, even though they're so important … life-changing, in fact).

But wait. What *is* a vaccine? A vaccine is a preparation that helps the body learn how to fight the germ that causes a certain disease.

Think of your body like a *dojo* – a place where you train in martial arts. The vaccine is like the Grandmaster. It takes a version or form of the germ that isn't as dangerous and introduces it into the body. The body's *immune system* then learns to create *antibodies* that can recognise the germ and fight it.

MEET YOUR OPPONENT.

ANTIBODY **VS** GERM

So, when the *real deal* shows up, the antibody knows *exactly* what to do with it.

These vaccinations protect them against all kinds of diseases such as measles, tetanus and polio (the antibody dojo has been *very* busy). Now, the recent COVID-19 pandemic has set things back a bit, making it harder to reach children all over the world. But all the organisations that have been doing so much good work here (such as Rotary, the World Health Organisation and the Bill and Melinda Gates Foundation) are doing their best to get things back on track as soon as they can.

SEE YA, SMALLPOX!

We actually *have* eradicated a disease before – smallpox. Smallpox caused mayhem all over the world for 3,000 years, killing hundreds of millions of people. Then, in 1796, a vaccine was developed. It took almost 200 years to finish the job, though. Things only really took off after the World Health Organisation came up with a GRAND PLAN in 1967. It played a huge part in getting countries to cooperate and taking care of things such as quality control. And by 1979, the world was declared smallpox-free! *Cooperation, see?* We get stuff done when we work together.

OFF YOU GO, POLIO!

Other vaccines are working too. We're so close to *eradicating* polio altogether:

- In 1988, there were 350,000 cases in 125 countries.
- By 2019, there were fewer than 40 cases, and they were found in just *two* countries.

THAT'S A DROP IN CASES OF OVER 99.9 PER CENT!

GAVI, THE VACCINE ALLIANCE

A huge chunk of progress on the vaccine front is thanks to organisations such as Rotary, the World Health Organisation, and the Bill and Melinda Gates Foundation. More recently, an organisation called Gavi has joined the cause too. Gavi is a global vaccine alliance that was set up in 2000 to help immunise children in lower-income countries to protect them against diseases like the ones we mentioned earlier. Gavi works with governments, researchers, vaccine manufacturers and charitable organisations and today, together with these partners, it helps vaccinate almost *half* the world's children. The funding it gets from wealthier countries helps make sure poorer countries can have the vaccines they need. As those countries get wealthier, *they* start putting money in the pot too. So everyone helps each other. *How lovely is that?*

'ALONE WE CAN DO SO LITTLE; TOGETHER WE CAN DO SO MUCH.'

HELEN KELLER, author, educator and disability rights activist

Led by Gavi, the World Health Organisation and a bunch of partners, over 190 countries got together in an effort to ensure fair access to vaccines for COVID-19 by sharing production and distribution costs. Because, it's not enough to *have* a vaccine – it needs to be able to reach the most vulnerable people all over the world. The pandemic has shown how connected we all are – it's not something any one country can fight alone. We *have* to work together.

CRANKING UP THE SPEED: Vaccines can take ten to 15 years to develop – sometimes more than that – but when the heat is on, scientists can act **FAST**. Look at how fast scientists all around the world got to work on the COVID-19 vaccine, involving millions of volunteers and moving from **NOTHING** to the first UK, EU and US-approved vaccine in under a year. That's *months* as opposed to years, or even *decades*! There's that incredible human creativity again and teamwork too!

GENOMICS
WHATOMICS?! Yep. That was my reaction too.

It's basically the study of the *genome,* and it's a big help in the fight against disease. Every organism has a genome – it's like an instruction manual on how to build you, and it's made up of something called DNA. As part of the Human Genome Project that started in 1990, scientists all over the world spent 13 years trying to understand the human genome and figuring out what order its

3 billion bits go in (like a ridiculously tricky LEGO pack where they forgot to slip in a step-by-step guide). Why, you might ask. Well, understanding the genome is the key to finding out if we're likely to get certain diseases like cancer, heart disease and diabetes. It means we can find out early and take action before things get worse. In the future, genomics might even help doctors tailor treatments just for us! This is called 'precision medicine' and it might change how medicine works forever.

'HEY, CAN SOMEONE GET ME A DOCTOR?'

Access to health care is so key. You can't look after people and keep them healthy if they can't get to a hospital and see a health professional. And those vaccines we chatted about aren't delivered by magical fairies. It takes some serious health heroes to do this stuff. So let's have a little look at some of them and the good things they've been doing:

VACCINATION WARRIORS: The polio vaccination project has brought together over 20 MILLION volunteers, doctors and nurses from all over the world. They've had to reach children who live in all sorts of places – from bustling cities to the deepest jungles and the remotest mountaintop villages. They've used everything from bikes and helicopters to camels and donkeys to get to them. How amazing is that?! Basically, if you can't get to health care, health care can come to **YOU!**

MEDICS ON WHEELS: We've got mobile health clinics everywhere from Zambia and Iraq to rural USA, getting into places where there aren't any hospitals for miles and miles. They've also travelled into

Syrian refugee camps and helped homeless people on the streets of London.

MEDICS ON MOBILE This is where health workers do check-ups and chats over video call, telephone or even by text message. Not just useful for people in remote places – it's been picking up in places such as Germany, the USA and China (because it's convenient, quick and easy) and it's actually proved to be *pretty* handy during a pandemic too!

HEALTH HEROES IN THE PANDEMIC

You'll probably have seen lots of these in action once COVID-19 started whizzing its way around the world. Nurses, doctors, care workers and other health workers worked around the clock – and at great risk to their own lives – to look after patients. In the UK, we call them **KEY WORKERS** – the ones we can't do without. Not just health workers, but also the shop workers and delivery people who kept supplies going, the people who collected bins, and the teachers who looked after the children of key workers while they went about their jobs. Sometimes it takes a big scary event like a pandemic to realise that some jobs out there are really so very important. The people who do them are **STARS** and often don't get paid nearly enough for what they do.

CHALLENGE Key workers do so much for us. Can you think of a creative way to thank them? A note? A picture? A poem? A song? Something to send to your local school or hospital or grocery store to show just how much you appreciate them?

MAKING HEALTH CARE AFFORDABLE

Health care is **PRICEY**. There are people out there who *need* medical treatment but can't afford it. And every year, around the world, 100 million people are tipped into extreme poverty because of their health care bills. This is where systems like the the National Health Service (NHS) in the UK step in and shine.

Set up in 1948 after the Second World War, the NHS is one of the best examples of a big project to make sure every citizen in the UK has free access to health care *all their life.* It was a rocky start, sure – they needed lots more staff and they had a huge queue of people waiting for medicines and treatment – but it's made a big difference. It means seeing a doctor, getting checked up, tested and operated on is all **FREE** when you need it. No, there's no magic money tree – it's all paid for by taxes. *Taxes* are a way of everyone in the country chipping in to a big pot (and those with more are supposed to chip in more than those with less). That tax money makes sure everyone has access to things such as schools, parks, roads, emergency services and hospitals so everyone has health care whenever they need it. No matter who they are, where they live or how much money they have. You need help, you get it.

The San Francisco Cuddle Club connects lonely elderly people with older dogs who might not be adopted because of their age. That means cuddles, company and a chance for a bit of gentle exercise too!

GOOD NEWS FLASH!

CLEAN WATER

Clean, safe water is a must if we're going to stop the spread of disease, but so many people around the world don't have access to it at all. Or they have to walk long and *dangerous* journeys just to get it.

The good news is that things *are* getting better. A report by the World Health Organisation and UNICEF shows that since 2000, at least 1.8 billion people have gained access to better sources of drinking water such as a piped connection.

Now, access to water in some parts of the world can still be patchy – maybe only for a few hours a day. It's not the 24/7 running water we might be used to! LUXURY, right?! But progress is progress. You've got to think about the *starting point* too. I mean, look at Ethiopia. It's managed to provide safe drinking water to 40 per cent of its population in just 25 years despite struggling with war, famine and a bunch of other local challenges. That's pretty impressive.

Paraguay's another example. About half the rural population had access to safe water in 2000. By 2017, it was 99 per cent. These guys were all over it. They even declared the right to water a human right three years before the UN did.

SCRUB THOSE PAWS: It might sound *really* obvious, but washing your hands with soap and water (and I mean a proper solid scrub!) makes a **MASSIVE** difference in stopping disease in its tracks. We've already seen how important it is in the fight against COVID-19. The thing is, only 60 per cent of people on the planet have access to basic handwashing facilities at home. So there's a mega-push to change that and companies such as Unilever have been chipping in too. Their Lifebuoy soap handwashing project has helped over 1 billion people all over the world, setting up handwashing stations, training local communities and making soaps affordable and easy to get hold of.

Charities are also doing lots to help, working with local communities to shake things up. Like in Nepal, where an organisation called 'charity: water' worked with a local partner, Nepal Water for Health, to build a pipe system capturing natural spring water high up in the mountains and delivering it down to tap stands in the Sindhuli district. Or in Madagascar, where WaterAid worked with a local group to build a new water system with 13 water points. When 85-year-old Dadabe, the oldest person in the village of Belavabary, turned on the new tap for the first time, he was so happy he celebrated by busting some dance moves!

But there's another big thing to sort out that's very *closely* connected to clean, safe water, and that's ... **SANITATION.**

In other words ...

TOILETS!

Toilets look different all over the world – from a hole in the ground to low ones and high ones. In some places, they can even give you a wash and sing you a song! But I'm talking *basic* toilet systems here. And what I really mean by that is some kind of safe waste-disposal system for human wee and poo. There. I said it. Safe disposal is key. When that isn't there, you're back to grappling with a whole bunch of nasty diseases as the water supply and local area become contaminated and … well, you get the picture!

So – *toilets.* We don't have anywhere near enough of them. Less than half the world's population has access to a safely managed sanitation service. And 673 million people still have to do their business *outside* in the open. Thankfully, governments, charities and local communities have been working so hard to bring these numbers down. They've done especially well in places such as Ethiopia, Bangladesh, Nepal, Pakistan and India.

MEET MR TOILET:

Seriously. This is Jack Sim, a Singaporean businessman who gave up his career to focus on campaigning for … **TOILETS!** He founded the World Toilet Organisation on 19 November 2001 to help educate and train people and basically change the world. He named that day World Toilet Day. Twelve years later, the UN made it an official day in their calendar. You can put it in yours too!

And there are more pieces of news to hang your hopes on. There are people out there trying to reinvent the whole thing to make sanitation more affordable so *everyone* can have access to it.

See, the toilet that you think of when I say 'toilet' is probably this one:

This beauty is based on technology that was invented in 1775. The toilet itself goes back way further – the Sumerians of Mesopotamia made early versions over 5,000 years ago, and there's evidence of toilets flushed with running water in the ancient Indus civilisation too. The system works just fine but the world's poorest can't afford the sewage structure it needs. So people are coming up with cheaper ideas. The Bill and Melinda Gates Foundation even ran a **TOILET CHALLENGE** to find the best invention! Among the prize-winners were a solar-powered toilet and a waterless *nano-membrane* toilet, which incinerates waste and may generate enough energy to charge a cell phone!

WHO KNOWS? Maybe an exciting new toilet design will make all the difference one day.

And *speaking* of innovations that could save lives … there's a lot happening in the world of technology, and it's worth a little peek!

LIFE-CHANGING TECHNOLOGY

TRACKERS AND WEARABLES:

You might have seen some of these around – some are worn like watches and track things such as the steps you take and your heartbeat. But they're not just a funky thing to help people get fit. They're *extremely* handy if you can't just pop into a hospital for a check-up. Or where a patient needs to be monitored.

DRONE DELIVERIES: Ever seen one of these? You might even have played with one! Drones are remotely piloted aircrafts and, unlike ambulances, they can get *everywhere*. So, they can get medical supplies to hard-to-reach places, delivering things such as medicines and test kits or picking up samples for a lab.

VIRTUAL REALITY (VR): Gaming, right?! NO! Well, not *just* gaming. VR can be used to train surgeons or to help existing ones practise tricky operations in super-realistic settings! Can you imagine? It might even help patients feel calmer by putting them in a really relaxing and comforting world. Good *music*. Comfy *setting*. So many possibilities!

3-D PRINTING: This has been used to print all sorts of things from personalised surgical tools to prosthetic (artificial) limbs. Basically, things that are often really expensive and take ages to make, or things that are needed urgently – such as protective kit in a pandemic! (3-D printing looks like it'll be BIG news. Wonder if we'll be able to 3-D-print ourselves a nice snack someday ...)

ARTIFICIAL INTELLIGENCE:

Scientists are looking into how *algorithms* can be created to do stuff such as diagnose (and even predict!) illnesses, even when they're really hard to detect. That's because these algorithms can process **HUMUNGOUS** amounts of data and spot patterns in it. It's not about replacing humans but *helping them to do their job!*

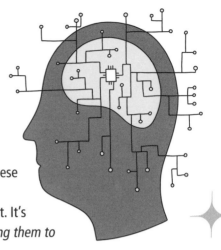

CHALLENGE How else do you think AI or robots could help with health care? Just picture it. What could the future look like?

GOOD NEWS FLASH!

A British company called Gravity Industries has teamed up with local paramedics to test a medical jet suit to help people in hard-to-reach hilly or rocky areas.

Health is a **BIG** and important area. We've got more global challenges than you can shake a stick at and the news makes everything look quite bleak. It's doing an important job though – don't knock it. It's showing us all the things we need to sort out. But if it's making you feel worried or overwhelmed ... good people on the case. Things may seem bad, but they are getting better and better thanks to our health heroes and lots of clever, creative, big-hearted people. One day, *you* might be one of them too!

WHAT'S LEFT TO DO

- We need to eradicate the diseases we can get rid of.
- We need to make sure *everyone* has access to clean water and sanitation (yes, TOILETS).
- We leave no one behind. Health care inequality is the biggest problem and it needs sorting out – where you are born or where you live shouldn't affect your right to treatment.
- We need to be clever about using funky technology, finding ways to make things cheaper, better and available to *everyone*.

HOW WE GET THERE – WHAT YOU CAN DO

READ UP: ... about health issues around the world. Fact-check stuff and apply all the fake news tests to make sure you're not dealing with any misinformation!

KEEP TALKING: ... about health issues with the people around you. But also keep talking about your health. We all have bodies and at some point we will all have broken bones, feel unwell or have to take a visit to the hospital. That's OK, and it's nothing to be scared of. Don't keep things bottled up. If you're worried about something – whether it's your body or your mind – talk to a trusted adult so they can help you.

SPEAK OUT: When you see something that's unfair – like some people having access to clean water and working toilets just because of where they live while other people don't have those things and can catch all kinds of diseases because of that – write to companies working in those areas to see if they're rolling their sleeves up and helping. Write to politicians to see if there's something they can do.

MAKE A CHANGE: You might be able to raise money to support projects that help fight disease and give people a chance to have cleaner water and safer sanitation. Maybe one day you'll design the next best thing in toilets or some other amazing piece of technology that saves lives. Or maybe you'll be a doctor, a nurse or another type of key worker, making a difference in people's lives every single day.

CHAPTER 5

GOOD SOCIETY

FAIRNESS, SPEAKING OUT AND SHAKING UP THE WORLD

Have you ever had that feeling that something is just not fair?! Like when you and a sibling or friend get caught doing something you shouldn't do (I mean, that'd never happen, but just imagine, OK?) and **YOU** get in trouble but the other person skips off into the sunset. Or imagine this: it's a boiling hot day and you go to buy an ice cream. But the ice-cream seller gives the person before you a **WAY** bigger helping of ice cream in their cone than they give you, just because they have green eyes and you don't. Or maybe you *do* have green eyes and *you* get the bigger ice cream while your brown-eyed buddy gets a much smaller one. How do you feel about that? Is it fair?

You might have heard a few people say things like, 'Yeah, well life isn't fair.' And they're right. Bad things – like illness and accidents – happen to 'good' people, and we'll never stop that happening. But some types of unfairness in the world *can* be fixed. You might have thought the green-eye example was really odd, but actually people *are* treated differently just because of how they look. Or where they're from. Or their health status. We'll come back to that unequal treatment point – it's a biggie! – but there's also a huge **GAP** between what some people have and how they live, and what *others* have and how *they* live.

!

THERE ARE GAPS *BETWEEN* COUNTRIES.

THERE ARE GAPS *WITHIN* COUNTRIES.

And I'm not just talking tiny gaps you can hop right over. I'm talking great big **GULFS.**

There are some people in the world with more money than they know what to do with and there are some who don't even know when they'll be able to have a proper meal or a safe place to sleep. They may not have access to basic things such as an education, clean water or health care. You might see a lot about this on the news. It's worrying and it's heartbreaking. But listen, we've come a long, long way with this as a human race and there are people dedicating their whole *lives* to making things better. I mean, things aren't exactly *peachy*, but there's no reason to tear up the whole report card. Look at the strides we're taking …

WE ARE COMMITTED TO TACKLING EXTREME POVERTY AND IT IS MAKING A DIFFERENCE.

Poverty levels have been falling across the world. Whaaaat? That's not what the papers say, right? That's probably because it's been a gradual improvement over time, not a big sudden change to make a splash in the news with. But it's REAL.

The 'poverty line' is the minimum level of income needed to get by. It's not perfect but it gives us some idea. Internationally, that line is set at US $1.90 a day and it helps us work out how many people are living in *extreme* poverty. That number has more than HALVED since 1990 (and – although it's hard to be sure of figures the further back you go – it's been falling steadily for the last *200 years*). Since 1990, a *billion* people have been lifted out of the most awful living conditions there are in the world.

Now, a lot of people say US $1.90 is nowhere *near* enough to live on and they're right. It absolutely isn't. There are some higher poverty lines too – like US $5 a day, US $7 a day or even US $15 a day.

The number of people living under **EVERY SINGLE ONE** of these lines has been falling as well. Until now ...

Unexpected global events, such as the COVID-19 pandemic, can push millions of people back into extreme poverty because of the job losses that come as a result. This means that we have to work harder in the fight against poverty. And that means ALL OF US ... governments, charities, businesses, individuals. We have come so far already and this is not the time to stop.

GOOD NEWS FLASH!

Manchester United footballer Marcus Rashford launched a campaign to stop children going hungry over the school holidays during the pandemic. Hundreds of local cafés, restaurants, shops, charities and local councils answered his call, offering free meals to disadvantaged children. How great is that! Individuals helped out too and spread the word about the cause, petitioning the government to do something to end child poverty.

ACROSS THE WORLD, MORE CHILDREN GO TO SCHOOL TODAY THAN EVER BEFORE. AND MORE GIRLS GO TO SCHOOL TODAY THAN EVER BEFORE.

Now you might be thinking, erm, why are you focusing on girls? But in the past, in most of the world, girls *couldn't* go to school (though there were a few exceptions, like ancient Sparta, where boys and girls got the same basic education – **HIGH-FIVE, SPARTANS!**). People thought education wasn't something girls needed to worry their pretty little heads over (can you imagine?).

Thankfully, we've taken some **BIG** steps in the last 200 years (and in the last 50 years especially). Now, most people realise how important it is for every child to have an education, not just boys. And with more boys and girls going to school, this means more children can read and write than ever before – which opens the door to so many more opportunities. And it's not just reading and writing – education is actually connected to **SO MANY** things ...

LIKE HEALTH: you learn how to take care of yourself and protect yourself against disease.

... UNDERSTANDING NATURE: you learn how the world works and where YOU fit in. You learn how to take care of the environment.

... AND BEING READY FOR LIFE: you learn about yourself. How to work with other people. And how to learn new things so that when you grow up, you can get a job or set up a business and earn money to help you and your family live a better life.

EDUCATION IS LIKE A KEY.

IT UNLOCKS OPPORTUNITIES.

'EDUCATION ISN'T A LUXURY; IT'S A LIFELINE. IT'S NOT A PRIVILEGE; IT'S A PRIORITY'

QUEEN RANIA AL ABDULLAH OF JORDAN,
activist and humanitarian

If you can read and write and know how to handle numbers, you can get jobs that need those skills. Often, those jobs pay a bit more. That's why **EQUALITY OF OPPORTUNITY** is important. That's the idea that we should all have a chance at doing OK. At the moment, *millions* of children around the world have the odds stacked so high against them, it's just not fair. Education can help change that. That's why it's important that it's free and available to *everyone*.

Sounds good, right? Well, here are some of the things people are doing to reach out to children who can so easily get left behind:

- The charity War Child have been training teachers and rehousing schools in conflict zones in Afghanistan and Yemen, bringing thousands of forgotten children back into the classroom.

- The LEGO Foundation's Education Cannot Wait campaign has helped to safely move and restart 40 schools destroyed by an accidental explosion in Beirut, Lebanon, in 2020.

- There are free school meal programmes all over the world in places such as the UK, Estonia, Sweden, Finland, Brazil, India and Liberia that give children one meal a day, keeping little tummies full and making a big difference to children whose families struggle to afford proper meals.

- Pan-African charity CAMFED (Campaign for Female Education) has been helping to get girls from rural parts of Ghana, Malawi, Tanzania, Zambia and Zimbabwe into school. They pay for things such as uniforms, books, bikes to get to school (because it's often far away), and glasses and hearing aids for children who can't study without them.

These are just a few examples, but there are so many people working on getting children into school. And, with the coronavirus having disrupted education for so many kids worldwide, it's more important than ever to support the organisations trying to make a change.

But what happens *next?* What happens after you leave school?

THE BIG BAD WORLD OF WORK

Now, school's cool, but you need some opportunities at the *end* of it, right? And there are people and organisations doing good things here too. Here are some great examples:

- Sebastián Salinas, whose social enterprise Balloon Latam helps disadvantaged people set up their own businesses in Chile, Argentina and Mexico.

- A UN project that trains up women in remote parts of Yemen to set up business, running their own solar-powered energy grids. It means they can help feed their families and bring power to rural areas at the same time.

- London-based charity Breaking Barriers, which has teamed up with Swedish furniture company IKEA to help refugees find jobs so they can rebuild their lives.

- Leila Janah (who sadly isn't around any more – she died from cancer in early 2020), whose business Samasource has helped 10,000 of the poorest people in Kenya, Uganda and India find very do-able digital jobs.

Imagine that. It's something to pop in your pocket for when people say **ALL** businesses are bad. They don't have to be. I'm sure if you set one up, it'd do some good in the world too. What do *you* think?

The bosses at 27 big businesses in New York – from tech and media to banking and health businesses – have promised to hire 100,000 New Yorkers from low-income and minority backgrounds by 2030.

GOOD NEWS FLASH!

THE FIGHT FOR EQUAL TREATMENT

So far, we've been thinking about inequality (or unfairness) in terms of money and how we live – including the basics such as health and education. But like we said earlier, there's another kind of inequality that affects so many of us. And that's to do with how we're treated.

You might think we're all human, so we'll all be treated the same. Right?

BUT WE'RE NOT.

Some people are treated differently because of their gender. Or because of the colour of their skin or where they're from. Or because of who they love. Or because they're disabled. And because of how they're treated, there are opportunities that might be closed to them when they shouldn't be. Or if not closed, really, *really, reeeeeally* difficult to access so basically … yep – *closed.*

But again, things *are* changing. Bit by bit. And those bits add up.

THE GENDER EQUALITY MOVEMENT

In the last few decades, all over the world, we've got:

- more girls going to school
- fewer girls being forced to get married early
- more women being able to vote and have a say in who makes the rules
- more women in politics and leadership roles in companies
- more laws in place to make sure women aren't treated badly just for being women.

We've also got people talking about the **GENDER PAY GAP.** That's the idea that some women get paid less than a man doing the *same* job.

Unbelievable, I know. But it **HAPPENS**. And more and more people are speaking out about it all over the world. Some companies are publishing information on what their workers get paid so

people can see it all out in the open. You have got to be able to see it if you're going to call it out and fix it! And, slowly, the gender gap is narrowing in many countries around the globe.

THE LGBTQ+ (LESBIAN, GAY, BISEXUAL, TRANSGENDER, QUEER) RIGHTS MOVEMENT

Some people are discriminated against because they're a woman in a relationship with a woman, a man in a relationship with a man or because they don't see themselves as fitting into a box that says they're a man or a woman. In the UK, for example, being gay used to be seen as a mental illness or something *really bad.* You could even be *imprisoned* for it. Mathematician Alan Turing's codebreaking work in the Second World War saved millions of lives but he was convicted for being in a relationship with a man and lost his job at the British secret service! What a way to thank a **HERO!** Thankfully, things are very different today and a lot of that is down to the LGBTQ+ rights movement.

These activists have fought for the right for everyone to live peaceful lives, to be able to love and marry whoever they want and to be free to be *themselves.* Seems pretty basic, doesn't it? But can you believe that up until 1967, in England and Wales it was illegal for two men to be in a relationship? And marriage between two men or between two women has only been allowed in England and Wales since 2013, 2014 in Scotland and 2020 in Northern Ireland. LGBTQ+ relationships are still criminalised in many countries but people are campaigning for that to be changed. Thanks to the hard work of activists around the world, more and more countries are gradually passing marriage-equality legislation.

Today, Pride parades are held across the world to mark the Stonewall uprising of 1969 when people stood up to police raiding a gay club in New York City. These parades are the most joyful celebrations of what it means to just be yourself – lots of rainbows, sparkles, music and jubilation! But the messages behind them are important ones – unity, self-acceptance and the commitment to campaigning for equality.

GOOD NEWS FLASH!

All Scottish state schools are required to teach LGBTQ+ history so everyone can grow up understanding the problems of discrimination, the struggle for equality and appreciating that families come in all shapes and forms. We are who we are, we love who we love and we all deserve to be treated fairly and with respect.

'WE PAVE THE SUNLIT PATH TOWARD JUSTICE TOGETHER, BRICK BY BRICK. THIS IS MY BRICK.'

TIM COOK, openly gay Chief Executive Officer of Apple

THE CIVIL RIGHTS MOVEMENT, 1950S AND 1960S, USA

Today, people are speaking out about racial equality all over the world. That's actually pretty amazing because at one time, in the world's most powerful countries, it was thought that some people's lives were worth more than others. That it was OK to *own* another human being. **SHOCKING**, right? But that's how the world looked just a couple of hundred years ago. During the transatlantic slave trade, over *12 million* African people were shipped from Africa over to the Americas (many of them on British ships) and those that survived the perilous journey were enslaved and put to work.

The majority of people thought that this was acceptable. A lot has changed since then and thank goodness for that. The transatlantic slave trade and slavery were abolished, for starters (by 1834 in Britain and by 1865 in the USA). And today, slavery is considered by practically everyone to be completely unacceptable. But there are still some issues from the past that need to change. Discrimination because of culture, race or skin colour is one of them.

Back in the 1960s, civil rights activists in the USA fought hard to end *segregation* – where Black people were forced to go to different schools, sit separately on buses and use different bathrooms to white people. In 1963, a quarter of a million Americans took part in the March on Washington to protest racial inequality. This is where Martin Luther King Jr made his famous 'I have a dream' speech. Well, all those voices made a difference. In 1964, the Civil Rights Act outlawed ANY discrimination on the basis of race, colour, sex, religion and origin in the US. (I mean, yeah, sounds super-obvious, but seems we needed an **ACTUAL LAW** to shake things up.)

These were incredible steps forward but they didn't end *racism*.
Black people were (and are!) still treated unfairly ... sometimes
even by the police.

THE BLACK LIVES MATTER MOVEMENT

In 2013 in the USA, a jury decided to let an armed civilian off the
hook after shooting and killing 17-year-old Trayvon Martin for
looking 'suspicious'. Trayvon was unarmed and headed back from
a shop where he had just bought some sweets and an iced tea. His
death sparked a movement – Black Lives Matter. Since the start of
this movement, many Black people have died at the hands of some
police officers and civilians. These deaths sparked public outrage.

In 2020, the same thing happened to an unarmed hospital worker
called Breonna Taylor. But when a man called George Floyd,
suspected of using a fake US$20 note, was held down by the police
and died in their custody, people decided enough was enough. And
the Black Lives Matter movement took off again in a big way with
protests and marches and petitions being signed *all over the world*.

KICKING OFF A GLOBAL CONVERSATION

Though this movement began in the USA, it reminded people
everywhere to think really deeply about racism in society. More and
more people are talking about it and calling it out – including things
such as Black people being discriminated against at work or at school
and not having the same chances in life as other people because of
it. Awareness is growing and the movement is getting bigger.

And the really powerful thing is that this global conversation isn't just about what's wrong in the world – it's a conversation about how to *fix* it. Some companies have been stepping up, promising to hire more Black people or helping them with cash to set up their own businesses or to go to school or college. Meanwhile, people everywhere are talking about this idea of being an *ally* ...

SEE IT, SORT IT. BE AN ALLY

Racial discrimination is still a big problem. Maybe you've experienced it too. Or maybe you've seen it happen around you and felt uncomfortable about it. And if you do see it, you might wonder what you can do. Well, you can BE AN ALLY – a genuine supporter.

Being an ally isn't just about protests, petitions and writing letters. It's also about doing things like:

- READING UP on what's happening (and why) and raise awareness about it. Learn about what you can do to help. What you can do better.

- LISTENING to people who are being treated unfairly.

- CHECKING IN on friends who might be having a hard time because of this – seeing if they're OK (but not expecting them to say anything because it might just be too much – just knowing you're there for them is the main thing).

- STICKING UP for other people and calling out racism whenever you see it.

- **CELEBRATING** Black people's achievements that often get forgotten! Lots of people credit Thomas Edison with inventing the commercial light bulb, but do they know that Black inventor **LEWIS LATIMER** invented the carbon filament that makes it work? Do they know it was a Black engineer called **JERRY LAWSON** that came up with the first video-game cartridge, making gaming consoles like Nintendo possible?! And so many people think of Florence Nightingale when they think of the most famous nurse in history, but do they know about pioneering British-Jamaican nurse **MARY SEACOLE?**

We need heroes and role models from everywhere. They exist but they don't always get enough airtime. We need to shout about them.

We're talking about one example here – the Black Lives Matter movement. But you can be an ally for any person or group of people facing discrimination, whether that's because of where they're from, who they love, their religion, because they're disabled or because they don't fit into some other box that the world expects them to fit into. You can check in on people, be there for them and raise awareness about discrimination. And you can read, celebrate and spread the word about the achievements of people from those backgrounds and groups. So everyone can see that *all* humans are capable of awesome things.

CLOSING GAPS AND ZOOOOMING IN ON THE GOOD STUFF

Inequality is a really tough area. We've got some **MEGA** gaps to deal with when it comes to income, how people live, how they're treated and the opportunities they have. These sorts of things hit the news a lot and it's easy to feel like there's not much to be hopeful about. But we have seen improvements. They just tend to take a very long time and they tend to be a bit gradual, so unless you're really looking, you might not notice them. But they matter. And some really good people have worked super-hard to get us where we are today and they're STILL doing their thing. The changes they've fought for have changed the lives of millions of people.

COULD WE SPEED THINGS UP? I REALLY, REALLY HOPE SO.

But the first step is acknowledging the good stuff. There are lots of voices raising awareness and speaking out against discrimination of all kinds. Great change has come about when we put our voices together. What's to stop us changing the world again?

?

WHAT'S LEFT TO DO

- A bigger push to get rid of extreme poverty.
- A final push to get ALL the world's children in school.
- Closing that gender pay gap.
- Actually, closing ALL the pay gaps – everyone should be paid the same if they're doing the same work.
- Raising awareness about issues such as gender inequality and racism, LGBTQ+ rights and the rights of disabled people.
- AND ON THAT NOTE – making sure no one is treated differently because of their gender, the colour of their skin, where they're from, who they love, who they are or because of their health conditions.
- Making the world and all the amazing opportunities in it accessible to everyone.

HOW WE GET THERE – WHAT YOU CAN DO

READ UP: Know what's going on – sniff out unfairness around you (you'll know it when you smell it … because it smells **BAAAD**). Get to know the history to understand why things are the way they are. And get to know what movements are happening around you too.

KEEP TALKING: Be an ally. Talk to the people around you about what's fair and what's not. Talk about how some people have a WAY tougher starting point than others and what that means for the rest of their life. Talk about how some people are treated differently. You may have people around you who don't even notice that this is happening because they're lucky enough not to experience that stuff in their life or to see it around them. But everyone needs to know it happens, because if you can't see it, you can't sort it out.

SPEAK OUT: If you see someone being treated badly, you can call it out and talk about why it's not OK. You can protest to support causes you care about and, again, write to companies and politicians who you think could be pulling their weight more.

MAKE A CHANGE: Today, maybe you'll just be there for people. Or give whatever you can (if you can) or fundraise for causes you care about. Maybe one day you'll be a big giver, giving away lots of money to reduce inequality in the world. Maybe one day you'll set up a business that gives opportunities to people who wouldn't normally find work so easily. Or you might end up working on projects that help lift people out of poverty or get children into school or make sure everyone is being treated fairly. How cool would that be? **EXTREMELY COOL** is the answer.

CHAPTER 6

GOOD ARTS

BALLET to BOLLYWOOD, VIRTUAL GALLERIES AND DOODLES THAT LIFT YOUR SPIRITS

OK. Arts and culture. I've got a soft spot for this topic because I'm a writer, an artist. This is *my* territory. You might hear people telling you that arts and culture are *going to the dogs.* I actually have no idea what that phrase really means – do you? I quite like dogs. But it's supposed to be a negative expression. It's like saying it's all going downhill.

WELL.

NOT FROM WHERE I'M STANDING, IT'S NOT.

Arts and culture are more exciting, varied and accessible than ever before. And they're more badly needed than ever before. They've always been important to us. Right from when the first humans discovered they could paint pictures out of red ochre and charcoal. Right from when language developed enough for us to tell *stories.*

REAL ONES: 'HEY, THERE'S A SABRE-TOOTHED TIGER BEHIND YOU!'

AND MADE-UP ONES: 'SO I HAD THIS DREAM ... '

Things just took off from there, really. We made music. We sang. We made ourselves clothes in different styles. We collected treasures (OK, in recent history, a lot of that was plain stealing, but that's another issue!). As communities developed, we came up with our own stories, rituals, beliefs and all the stuff that comes with that. When we travelled, we took some of that with us and shared it around. And yes, when some groups of people took over other lands, some things got picked up and blended into other cultures that way too. Some art even developed in really difficult times as a way of making sense of things, documenting things or lifting people up. Today, the world is so connected we get to see and enjoy and learn from *all* of that.

IF YOU THINK
ABOUT IT ...
THAT.
IS.
MIND-BLOWING.

But it's not all smooth sailing. Some people say arts and culture are elitist or snobby and not for everyone. There's also the challenge of *paying* for all this stuff because it's often slightly lower down the list when it comes to prioritising what to spend on. And you can understand that – as much as I love the arts, if you're a country with huge environmental, health, education and inequality issues … you're going to need to pump money into those.

During the COVID-19 pandemic, arts venues and artists struggled a lot with fewer people out and about spending on these things – and it will take time for a lot of these places to recover. In fact, artists tend to struggle a lot. You might think of the big ones like Will Smith, Selena Gomez and Jeff Kinney (of Wimpy Kid fame!) who are doing OK, but for every one of those, there are millions of up-and-coming artists who find it really hard to pay their bills and just get by. And that's true for all kinds of artists – from actors and dancers to musicians and writers. So it's not all shiny happy stuff.

BUT … it's Chapter 6, so you know the drill now with this book.

We focus on the **HOPE** – the good things that are happening.

Let's start with this: **ART HAS ALWAYS SURVIVED.**

I just said that art tends to be low down on the list of priorities when it comes to spending and that lots of artists are struggling and it's all true. But somehow, *despite* that, the arts are still here. They've survived terrible recessions. In Nazi Germany, books were burned and some types of art were banned, but it survived. There were people who kept it alive. *Secretly.* Art has even survived **WARS**. How? What do you think? Maybe it's something to do with how very human art is, how important it is; to us. Early humans created cave paintings and told stories. It's what we do, isn't it? Can you even begin to imagine a world without stories or music or dance or art? Tell you what – I definitely can't. No wonder art has survived. We **NEED** it.

And actually, art hasn't just *survived*. In many ways, it's been **BOOMING** …

WE'VE GOT MORE CHOICE THAN EVER BEFORE

MOVIES ARE BOOMING: Not just Hollywood but other places such as the film industry in China and Bollywood in India. Did you know that *Nollywood* in Nigeria is cranking out over a thousand films a year? We're spending more money and time on films and TV shows than ever before, especially with online streaming.

MUSIC IS BOOMING: There's more music being released around the world each year than ever before. Today, we've got **SEVEN TIMES** more music releases around the world than we had in the 1960s. All kinds of music. The choice is incredible.

GAMING IS BOOMING: The global gaming industry is bigger than the music and film industries put together! Around a third of the world's population play video games. And now it attracts all kinds of people. Have you heard of Hamako Mori from Japan? Known as 'Gamer Grandma', she was born in 1930 and played her first video game in 1981. After that she was *hooked* and by the time she was 90, she was a proper YouTube star with hundreds of thousands of subscribers on her gaming channel.

BOOKS ARE BOOMING: The choice out there is **AMAZING.** Comics, graphic novels, poetry, fiction, factual books. There's something for everyone. We've even got things like e-books and audiobooks, which make reading (*and yes, it ALL counts as reading*) even more accessible for people who struggle with or don't have space for physical books.

Some of these areas in the entertainment industry (such as cinema and live music) have taken a hit because of the COVID-19 pandemic. But the experts say they'll boom again because we love them. We *need* them.

A *LITTLE* WORD ABOUT PIRACY ... You might discover that you can get some of this stuff for free online and think – wahoo – free stuff! But remember, someone has had to make that free game or that free movie, and by you downloading it (illegally, I may add), they're missing out on money. Which isn't fair. Don't be a pirate. They're not as cool as you think.

ARTS AND CULTURE ARE MORE ACCESSIBLE THAN EVER

There used to be (and actually there still is) this sense that arts and culture are just for the rich. I mean, just look at the term 'THE ARTS'. 'CULTURE'. It's got a certain flavour and feel to it, hasn't it? What does it make you think of? Fancy ballet performances, concerts and theatre shows? Priceless paintings in big, intimidating galleries?

It used to be the case that you needed to spend quite a bit of money to access many of these things. And maybe you had to be a certain type of person to feel like you fitted into that world. But that's CHANGING.

> IN FACT, YOU CAN DO SO MUCH OF THIS STUFF RIGHT FROM THE COMFORT OF YOUR SOFA!

Google Arts and Culture lets you step inside museums and galleries and visit cultural hotspots all over the world. There are countless shows about travel and history and lots of concerts, plays and comedy performances being beamed everywhere through our TVs.

There's actually always been some stuff that's cheap as chips or even FREE. In many countries, you'll find free or really cheap tickets for museums and galleries. And some countries have free library services. They are under threat in some parts of the world (including the UK) – libraries especially – but where they are available, imagine the difference they make. They help fight inequality too – *everyone* gets to learn about and explore the world. *Everyone.*

ART FOR EVERYONE

There's been a big movement to make the world more accessible for disabled people too. It's this idea that people aren't *disabled* by their medical conditions, they're *disabled* by *society* with all its barriers and attitudes. So that's what we should focus on changing. Lots of arts venues, for example, have been making sure they're more welcoming and enjoyable for disabled people. Especially because not all disabilities can be spotted from the outside. Some are hidden. Invisible. You never really know what someone's dealing with, so it's easier and kinder to just design a world that works for all of us!

Disability rights activist Dr Victor Pineda says we should always ask ourselves, 'Hey, what can we do to make this place more accessible? What can we do to make this place more inviting?' In the case of the arts, the answer is – *lots* of things. Such as adding subtitles and sign language to films, offering audio and Braille guides, adding lifts and accessible toilets to museums and galleries and making arts venues easier for everyone to get into. But also things such as keeping exhibits at a level that everyone can see and offering quiet spaces or quiet viewing hours for people who need them. We're seeing this more and more now – hopefully, one day, it'll be the norm everywhere.

'WE NEED TO MAKE EVERY SINGLE THING ACCESSIBLE TO EVERY SINGLE PERSON WITH A DISABILITY.'

STEVIE WONDER, musician, songwriter and civil rights activist

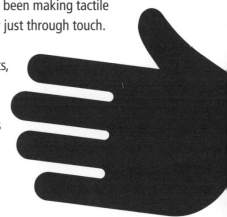

ART YOU CAN TOUCH

Some artists, companies and charities have been making tactile art and picture books – ones you can enjoy just through touch. Just as the invention of Braille made books readable for people with visual impairments, tactile art means that everyone can enjoy pictures and paintings. Remember what we said in Chapter 1? When kindness and compassion meet creativity, we humans come up with some really beautiful things to help each other.

GOOD NEWS FLASH!

A Hungarian orchestra helps deaf and hard of hearing people enjoy Beethoven's music – by touching the instruments, using balloons that capture the vibrations or using special hearing aids.

CHALLENGE How would you make the arts even more accessible? Got any ideas? What would help them reach everyone, no matter who they are, where they're from, where they live or how much money they have, and regardless of whether or not they're disabled? Because the arts are for *all* of us.

ART IS ALSO MORE INCLUSIVE THAN IT'S EVER BEEN

Art isn't just about the fancy few any more. It's not just posh poetry and paintings. It's punchy spoken word and rap – that's ART. It's clever verse novels by people such as Jason Reynolds and Margarita Engle. It's graffiti by people such as Banksy and KAWS. Who'd have thought that *street art* would sell for millions?

But hold on. Not everyone can AFFORD to make art. The fact is, like we said earlier, most of the time these sorts of jobs – amazing as they are – don't pay much. There's a lot of waiting for lucky breaks, a lot of slogging for very little pay. That's why *sometimes* you'll see richer people in the arts. Because they can afford to do what they love. But that's a big problem – every talented artist should be able to make art if they want to, and money shouldn't be a barrier. That's why there are organisations such as the Arts Council in the UK and the National Endowment for the Arts in the USA, which help support struggling artists and bust down those barriers.

Some galleries are making an extra push to showcase artists you might not normally see. The Museum of Modern Art (MoMa) in New York City mixed up its collection of classics such as Picasso and Van Gogh to highlight work by women artists and Black, Asian and Latin American artists.

When you look for a dance class, yes, you'll see ballet, but chances are you'll also see things such as Bollywood, bhangra, hip hop and salsa. If you're into music, you can listen to stuff from ALL OVER THE WORLD – from Jamaican reggae, Latin music and rock to Arabic music and K-pop from South Korea.

141

We've got stories from everywhere. Fashion influences from everywhere. And of course, food from everywhere too. Not just in restaurants (or pop-ups and roadside cafés) but in cookbooks, cookery shows on TV and clips on YouTube!

One of the many, **MANY** cool things about this is that it brings the world a bit closer together. We learn more about and appreciate different cultures, which makes life so much more exciting.

ART FILLS US WITH HOPE

When you're feeling a bit down or if you're stressed out, music, a good book or film can just take you away. It's uplifting. Some people find dancing does that. Or drawing. Or painting. Or colouring. It's really personal, but it can be such a comfort. Such as the uplifting murals in refugee camps or peaceful art in hospitals. Some artists have even painted the most fascinating pictures on MRI scanners and put them all around the hospital room to help young children stay *very* still while their brains are being scanned.

ART THERAPY

Have you heard of this? It's becoming more and more of a thing. It's where specially trained professionals use creative activities such as doodling, drawing, colouring, painting, sculpting, dance and music to help people express themselves and their feelings in a safe space and make sense of things. It won't work for everyone all the time, but some clever people are studying how it might help make a difference, bringing down stress levels, helping people to open up and deal with difficult feelings and improve their mental health.

> **'THE ONLY THING I KNOW IS THAT I PAINT BECAUSE I NEED TO.'**
>
> FRIDA KAHLO, Mexican artist

GOOD NEWS FLASH!

In 2019, when Chelsea Phaire was 10 years old, she started collecting art supplies and donating art kits to children in hospitals, foster homes and homeless shelters. 'Chelsea's Charity' has so far sent out over 2,500 of these kits.

Art brings people together too. Imagine a bunch of people all over the world bopping along to the same rhythm. Singing together. Feeling the same things. Or chatting away about a film or show and that *scene* that was just **SOOO GOOOOD.**

Art gets people talking.

It also gets them talking about *issues* ...

TACKLING SOCIAL INJUSTICE

Art has always been like a mirror, reflecting what's happening at the time it's created. It's a piece of history, in a way. And some art is specifically designed to make you think. Or to raise awareness about important issues. Like the work of Lebanese-American artist Helen

Zughaib, who raises awareness about protests and civil war in the Middle East. Or *Etnias* ('Ethnicities' in Portuguese), the GIANT mural painted by Brazilian artist Eduardo Kobra for the 2016 Olympics in Rio de Janeiro. It's about as tall as *three* giraffes and represents five indigenous tribes from five continents (inspired by the five Olympic rings). Kobra says he made the mural because he 'wanted to show that everyone is united; we are all connected'.

Music can be a kind of activism too. There are songs that raise issues such as homelessness, poverty, racism, disease and war. Books, plays, films and even dance can do the same. That's why some people throughout history have tried to control them and ban them if they didn't like what they said about the world. Art is powerful. And now, with the Internet, with travel, it can reach so many people and *super-*fast at that.

CHALLENGE Can you SAY IT WITH ART? Can you paint a picture, write a poem or song or create a sculpture about an issue you care about? To raise awareness about it. Or even just for you, to express how you feel.

> 'IF YOU ASK ME WHAT I CAME TO DO IN THIS WORLD, I, AN ARTIST, WILL ANSWER YOU ... I CAME HERE TO LIVE OUT LOUD.'
>
> ÉMILE ZOLA, writer and political activist

WE'RE ALL ARTISTS NOW

YouTube and other social media platforms have been GAME-CHANGERS. Now we can all learn how to sing, dance, play instruments, speak other languages, design, cook, paint. Anything we want, really. And in this new world, even small-town stars get a chance to shine. Everyone can be a poet, a singer, a dancer, an actor, a chef and an illustrator. But it's not all about fame. So much of this is about the way it makes us feel. It's a way of expressing ourselves. Even getting to know ourselves. And connecting with others.

We've redefined what art is. It's not just the elite stuff. It includes artists of all kinds and from all over the world. That's something exciting. Yes, art is struggling money-wise. It's had this problem throughout history – that's nothing new. But it has survived. Because it matters. And it will survive. We'll do whatever it takes to make sure it does.

WHAT'S LEFT TO DO

- Better funding for the arts, including for struggling artists, because *everyone* should be able to fulfil their artistic potential and money should not be a barrier.

- More work on making the arts accessible to everyone – including disabled people.
- Greater recognition that arts and culture *matter* and make a difference.
- More recognition of the role of arts and culture in calling out injustice, lifting people up and giving them hope and comfort and a safe space to express themselves!

HOW WE GET THERE – WHAT YOU CAN DO

READ UP: Go to your local library and read about different art movements and artists. Maybe you'll discover an artist you didn't know before and you could try out their style – have a go at collaging like Henri Matisse or painting with your fingers like Georges-Pierre Seurat. Get inspired, expand your horizons, be curious and read lots – hey you're reading this book so that's a start!

KEEP TALKING: If you hear about an arts venue closing or artists struggling because money or funding is tight, help them raise awareness. Without a bit of love and support, maybe only the big guys will survive and that would be sad. When you spread the word, you might encourage more people to support them too.

SPEAK OUT: If you can think of ways to make the arts more accessible to people, speak out about it. Maybe you visit a museum but it's full of steps and crowds and teeny-tiny writing that people with visual impairments find hard to read. Let them know! And speak out if you think a venue or club needs to be more inclusive, too. Are they only showcasing a certain type of artist? Are some people and cultures being missed out? Could you do something to get the word out?

MAKE A CHANGE: Support artists and creatives and clubs and venues that aren't very well known – they need ALL the help they can get! Help them fundraise if you can. If you love them, tell them you do (trust me – this means a **LOT**). Tell other people you love them so they'll go out and visit them or check out their stuff. Visiting galleries or museums, buying books, watching plays, writing amazing reviews – it all counts. One day you might be able to give big to the arts. You might run an arts venue (and if you do, I bet you'll do everything in your power to make it accessible and inclusive). You might **BECOME** an artist. You might be one already. And maybe, just maybe, you'll change the world through your art too.

WHAT'S NEXT?

RIGHT.

How was *that* for a whirlwind tour of the world?

More importantly ... how are you feeling about it all?

Hopefully, the answer to that is that you feel **HOPEFUL**.

The news is jam-packed with sad and scary stuff, and it can make the world look so much worse than it actually is. But now you know why. It's juicy. It grabs people's attention. It sells. And it's not just *bad* news. You have to deal with **FAKE NEWS** too. It's everywhere and it can whoosh round the world in no time at all. But you know how to sniff that out, right? You've got all the tricks now. And you've got your gut.

You've also got the facts and you know where to find more of them. And the facts tell us that, yes, this planet of ours needs quite a bit of work – but we've actually come a long way already. And that's easy to miss when there's so much bad news flying around. But that isn't going to fool you. Because you've seen that this world is full of good people doing good things and there's actually a lot of **GOOD NEWS** out there.

Good news about ...

... **HUMANS:** We're good at heart. We feel for others even when they're very different to us. We're kind, and tragedy brings out the best in us. We're creative and we can put that to good use. And we *want* to make a difference so chances are, when it comes to the crunch, we will.

... **POLITICS:** Activism is on the rise and it's changing the world. People have been fighting for – and winning! – the right to vote, we have more under-represented people in power than we've ever had, and while countries have their differences, they actually team up to do some pretty amazing things here on Earth (and in space too!).

... **THE PLANET:** We've figured out what the big problems are and what we should do about them **(PHEW!)**. We're tackling carbon emissions. We're working on listening more to indigenous people who know all about living in sync with nature. We've got clean energy options such as solar and wind power and they're getting cheaper and more powerful by the day. We're planting trees, walking, cycling and using more and more electric cars. We're **CLEANING** up and **GREENING** up.

... **HEALTH:** More people have access to clean water and sanitation all over the world than ever before (toilets are so important). We're tackling diseases, cracking the code to human DNA and using advanced technology such as 3-D printing and even virtual reality to improve health care.

... **SOCIETY:** We're tackling global poverty and it's making a difference. We have more people – including girls – in school than ever before. We've come a long way in terms of women's rights and LGBTQ+ rights. We're speaking out about these things. We're speaking out about racism. Things are shifting. They'll keep shifting.

... **ARTS AND CULTURE:** We're *flooded* with choice. There are more books, movies, shows, theatre, dance, comedy and music performances than you can shake a stick at! And thanks to the Internet, TV and smartphones, so many of us can enjoy these things while sitting at home in our PJs, stocked up with our favourite snacks. Even the really fancy stuff. Entertainment is more inclusive than it's ever been too – we get films from everywhere, music from everywhere, food from everywhere! And with platforms such as YouTube, *everyone* can learn stuff. Everyone can *create* stuff. Everyone can be a poet, a singer, a dancer, an actor, an artist.

There are so many good people doing amazing things, and by seeking them out and shouting about them, we keep all that good stuff in the spotlight where it belongs. Because good stuff inspires *more* good stuff.

Again, to be clear, this doesn't mean there aren't still a whole bunch of things that need fixing and shaking up around here. There are. (And there's space for us to do some of that fixing. A little bit now, whenever and wherever we can, and maybe some bigger and **BOLDER** things in the future too.)

It just means that ...

THE WORLD ISN'T SO BAD.

PEOPLE AREN'T SO BAD.

THERE'S HOPE.

WE JUST NEED TO KNOW WHERE TO LOOK FOR IT.

But don't take my word for it. Listen to American actor, director and activist Christopher Reeve. He was famous for playing Superman in the 1970s and 1980s but in 1995, he fell off his horse during a competition and injured his spinal cord so badly that he was paralysed from the neck down. He became a powerful advocate for disabled people, raising awareness and setting up a foundation to raise funds for research on spinal cord injury, helping to forge medical breakthroughs. This is what he said:

'ONCE WE CHOOSE HOPE, EVERYTHING IS POSSIBLE.'

CHRISTOPHER REEVE, American actor, director and activist

KEY SOURCES

We talked about the importance of using reputable, trustworthy sources. We've used lots of those to research this book (as you might have noticed, it's jam-packed with facts!). They include organisations such as the United Nations, the World Bank, the World Health Organisation, Statista and Our World in Data. Their researchers spend a lot of time studying the world and analysing the data so we can see exactly what is going on. Here are just some of the sources we've used for this book. You might want to use these someday too:

Beltekian, Diana and Ortiz-Ospina, Esteban. 'Extreme poverty is falling: How is poverty changing for higher poverty lines?' Our World in Data, 5 March 2018. https://ourworldindata.org/poverty-at-higher-poverty-lines, accessed 12 January 2021.

Roser, Max. 'Democracy – Number of Democracies.' Our World in Data. [June 2019] https://ourworldindata.org/democracy#number-of-democracies, accessed 12 January 2021.

Schaeffer, Katherine. 'Key facts about women's suffrage around the world, a century after U.S. ratified 19th Amendment.' Pew Research Center. 5 October 2020. https://www.pewresearch.org/fact-tank/2020/10/05/key-facts-about-womens-suffrage-around-the-world-a-century-after-u-s-ratified-19th-amend-ment/, accessed 12 January 2021.

Tiseo, Ian. 'Greenhouse gas emissions worldwide – Statistics and Facts.' Statista, September 2020. https://www.statista.com/topics/5770/global-greenhouse-gas-emissions/, accessed 12 January 2021.

UNICEF. 'Education: Every child has the right to learn.' https://www.unicef.org/education, accessed 12 January 2021.

United Nations Millennium Development Goals. https://www.un.org/millenniumgoals/, accessed 12 January 2021.

United Nations Sustainable Development Goals. https://www.un.org/sustainabledevelopment/sustainable-development-goals/, accessed 12 January 2021.

United Nations. 'The Climate Crisis – A Race We Can Win.' https://www.un.org/en/un75/climate-crisis-race-we-can-win, accessed 12 January 2021.

United Nations. 'World is closer than ever to seeing polio disappear for good.' UN News, 24 October 2019. https://news.un.org/en/story/2019/10/1049941, accessed 12 January 2021.

The World Bank. World Population. https://data.worldbank.org/indicator/SP.POP.TOTL, accessed 12 January 2021.

World Health Organisation and UNICEF. 'Progress on household drinking water, sanitation and hygiene 2000-2017: Special focus on inequalities.' World Health Organisation and UNICEF joint report, 2019. https://washdata.org/sites/default/files/documents/reports/2019-07/jmp-2019-wash-households.pdf, accessed 12 January 2021.

QUOTES (IN ORDER OF APPEARANCE)

Nelson Mandela. Address during Maskakhane Focus Week, Bothaville, South Africa, 14 October 1998. https://www.un.org/en/events/mandeladay/assets/pdf/mandela100-booklet.pdf, accessed 12 January 2021.

Michelle Obama. Remarks by The First Lady during Keynote Address at Young African Women Leaders Forum, 22 June 2011. https://obamawhitehouse.archives.gov/the-press-office/2011/06/22/remarks-first-lady-during-keynote-address-young-african-women-leaders-fo, accessed 12 January 2021.

Alexandria Ocasio-Cortez. 'Best of 2019 – When Alexandria Ocasio-Cortez met Greta Thunberg: 'Hope is contagious'. 29 June 2019. https://www.theguardian.com/environment/2019/jun/29/alexandria-ocasio-cortez-met-greta-thunberg-hope-contagious-climate, accessed 12 January 2021.

Autumn Peltier. 'Meet Autumn Peltier: 15-year-old internationally recognized clean water advocate and the Anishinabek Nation chief water commissioner', 5 November 2019. https://www.womenofinfluence.ca/2019/11/05/meet-autumn-peltier-14-year-old-internationally-recognized-clean-water-advocate-and-the-anishinabek-nation-chief-water-commissioner/, accessed 12 January 2021.

Kofi Annan. UN Press Release: Secretary-General Emphasizes Important Role of United Nations for New Millennium. 15 December 1999. https://www.un-.org/press/en/1999/19991215.sgsm7262.doc.html, accessed 12 January 2021.

Neil deGrasse Tyson. Twitter, 31 July 2012. https://twitter.com/neiltyson/status/230345104433500161?lang=en, accessed 12 January 2021.

Sir David Attenborough. BBC World Service's *The Arts Hour*, 5 January 2019. https://www.bbc.co.uk/sounds/play/w3cswq0y, accessed 12 January 2021.

Helena Gualinga. COP25 Press Conference - Indigenous Women from the Amazon: Calls to Action. 21 December 2019. https://www.wecaninternational.

org/post/people-power-rises-for-climate-justice-at-cop25, accessed 12 January 2021.

Dr Jane Goodall. 2018 Global Citizen Festival speech. https://news.janegoodall.org/2018/10/01/6539/, accessed 12 January 2021.

Anne Frank. Anne Frank's *Tales From The Secret Annexe.* Translated by Susan Massotty. (Halban: 2012)

Helen Keller. Helen and Teacher: *The Story of Helen Keller and Anne Sullivan Macy* by Joseph P. Lash. (AFB Press: 1980).

Marcus Samuelsson. UNICEF Tap Project, 2011. https://www.unicefusa.org/stories/how-unicef-tap-project-brought-safe-water-over-500000-people/30643, accessed 12 January 2021.

Queen Rania Al Abdullah of Jordan. Speech at 2016 Global Citizen Festival, 24 September 2016. https://www.globalcitizen.org/en/content/gucci-chime-for-change-promote-gender-equality-201/, accessed 12 January 2021.

Ruth Bader Ginsburg. Quote from the US case Reed vs Reed, 404 US, 1971. https://ukhumanrightsblog.com/2020/09/25/a-lifes-work-justice-ruth-bader-ginsburg-ruby-peacock/, accessed 12 January 2021.

Cook, Tim. 'Tim Cook speaks up'. Bloomberg, 30 October 2014. https://www.bloomberg.com/news/articles/2014-10-30/tim-cook-speaks-up, accessed 12 January 2021.

Stevie Wonder. The 58th Grammy Awards, 15 February 2016. https://www.youtube.com/watch?v=V-A9aajfcbU, accessed 12 January 2021.

Frida Kahlo. *The Biography of Frida Kahlo,* by Hayden Herrera. (Bloomsbury: 2018), p. 254.

Èmile Zola. *Mes Haines* by Émile Zola (Editions Flammarion: 2012), p. 62.

Christopher Reeve. *Nothing is Impossible: Reflections on a New Life* by Christopher Reeve. (Ballantine Books: 2002, NY edition).

INDEX